How to Become a SuperStar Student, 2nd Edition

Michael Geisen, M.A.

PUBLISHED BY:

THE GREAT COURSES
Corporate Headquarters
4840 Westfields Boulevard, Suite 500
Chantilly, Virginia 20151-2299
Phone: 1-800-832-2412
Fax: 703-378-3819
www.thegreatcourses.com

Printed in the United States of America

Michael Geisen, M.A.

2008 National Teacher of the Year

Professor Michael Geisen has been helping students in Oregon experience the wonders of science since 2001. In 2008, while teaching at Crook County Middle School in Prineville, Oregon, he was selected from among millions of public school educators to serve as the United States National Teacher of the Year. The National Teacher of the Year program is designed to highlight great teaching, learning, and leading, and Professor Geisen was honored to serve as an ambassador for the teaching profession during his year of service. He traveled full time both nationally and internationally, helping educators, policy makers, and community members find a better balance that truly meets the needs of students in a rapidly changing world.

Professor Geisen's approach in and out of the classroom is to teach main concepts using multiple learning pathways to reach all of his students. He uses movement, humor, music, technology, project-based learning, cooperative groups, art, theater, and personal connections with his students to make science fun and relevant to students' lives. His curriculum, labs, assignments, activities, and evaluations are hand-tailored, bringing together creativity and science. By creating his own curriculum and learning activities, Professor Geisen is able to correlate them to any state standards, incorporate multiple levels of cognition, revise them each year, and keep them up-to-date with emerging science.

During Professor Geisen's tenure at Crook County Middle School, students began achieving at unprecedented levels in science. Not only have they begun scoring among the state's best on traditional measures of achievement, but students in this low-income, rural community are demonstrating their learning in more hands-on ways—and loving science, too.

Professor Geisen earned his bachelor's degree magna cum laude from the University of Washington in Forest Resource Management. He had never really considered a career in teaching, planning on a career in graphic design and later geology before settling on forest management. But after working for several years as a professional forester, Professor Geisen realized that he wasn't all that passionate about what he was doing for a living. Although he loves the outdoors, he needed a better reason to get out of bed in the morning and more interaction with human beings. So he went back to school, earning his master's degree in Education at Southern Oregon University.

Professor Geisen found teaching to be a much better fit for his personality, passion, and skills than his previous career. While he still had to drag himself out of bed each morning, he did so knowing that he had the honor of affecting hundreds of lives each day. "It's an honor, and a great challenge," Professor Geisen states. "Every child is different, and every day is different; that's what makes teaching so captivating and challenging. That's what gets me out of bed in the morning, and it's why I collapse into bed each night!"

While Professor Geisen often jokes that he is the "greatest teacher to ever walk the face of the earth," he knows that it would impossible for anyone to make such a claim. Not only is great teaching too complex to measure simply, but it is also incredibly diverse in its manifestation, and every teacher is part of a larger community of educators working in collaboration.

Professor Geisen has taught students of all ages from elementary school to college but has spent the majority of his career in the middle grades. Most educators bestow "Navy Seal" status on middle school teachers, but Professor Geisen has always maintained that there is nothing all that scary about middle school students. While legend has it that as a forester he scared away a charging black bear (by hitting himself in the head with a stick), there have been no documented accounts of 7th graders charging him yet—at least, not without permission.

Professor Geisen has served on numerous state- and national-level commissions and panels and has been featured in dozens of books, articles, and media appearances. In addition to his acclaim as the National Teacher of the Year, he was selected as the 2009 Outstanding Teacher in K-12 Education by the Oregon Academy of Sciences, honored as the 2009 Toshiba Innovator in Education, and named the 2007–2008 Oregon Teacher of the Year.

Professor Geisen added a new facet to his career as an educator by becoming a full-time educational consultant. He now teaches fellow educators, policy makers, and businesspeople around the world about high-quality teaching and learning. His innovative and humorous approach has been widely acclaimed for helping people of all ages understand and apply big concepts in education and science. He currently spends much of his time working on creative curriculum development, writing, and working with teachers to improve their practice. He is well known around the United States for his engaging keynotes and workshops for educators, parents, and students.

Professor Geisen seeks a balanced, creative, and inquisitive life while not teaching, as well. He is an accomplished photographer, a mediocre musician, a climber, a lover of wild places, a husband, and a father. He loves to explore the world through the heightened senses of his children, Aspen and Johanna, whom he admires as his greatest teachers. ■

Table of Contents

INTRODUCTION

STUDENT LECTURE GUIDES

Table of Contents

How to Become a SuperStar Student, 2nd Edition

Scope:

The number one problem facing many high school students is that they haven't been taught how to learn. Because schools often focus on improving students' standardized test results, few students are deliberately taught about learning—about developing the particular mind-set and skills that can help them graduate not just with exemplary grades but with an exemplary mind.

Your professor, Michael Geisen, the 2008 National Teacher of the Year, has spent his career showing thousands of students these skills. In this set of 12 lectures for students and 6 lectures for parents, he'll teach you, too.

If you're a student …

… don't worry, this won't be a boring slog. First of all, you don't get to be Teacher of the Year with monotonous mumbling. Professor Geisen will keep your attention by being funny, informative, and useful—even all three at the same time. The course is packed with cool facts, great tools, and chances to practice using them in your own way, on your own terms.

Some of you might be nervous that this course will be way over your head. Maybe you think you can't be a superstar student. You can. Anyone can. The secret is to figure out your strengths and weaknesses and then determine what works best for you. You'll learn how to set *your* goals, figure out *your* priorities, develop *your* systems, and—most importantly—how to do all this and still have time for fun.

The 12 lectures for students begin by helping you figure out your own learning style, which will help you choose the tools and systems that are right for you. You'll then look at different ways to perform all sorts of school-related tasks, from the basic (taking notes, studying, writing papers) to the not-so-basic (planning, scheduling, group work, critical thinking).

Throughout the lectures, you'll also learn about how to better manage your life outside of school so you can be a superstar at everything you want to do.

If you're a parent …

… this course has six lectures designed just for you. Professor Geisen will help you figure out how you can help your children succeed, including when to take a step back. You'll learn effective strategies for dealing with your children's teachers, too—how to communicate and cooperate with them to make the most of your children's education. You'll get advice on preparing your children for college and careers, as well as how to raise them to have balance, confidence, and humility. As Professor Geisen says, "You're the person who knows your child best. Therefore, you need to be an integral part of the process." ■

Student Lecture Guides

Understanding Your Unique Intelligence
Lecture 1

Topics in This Lecture

- What is intelligence?
- How we're each unique: the different types of intelligence
- How we're all alike: characteristics that all students share

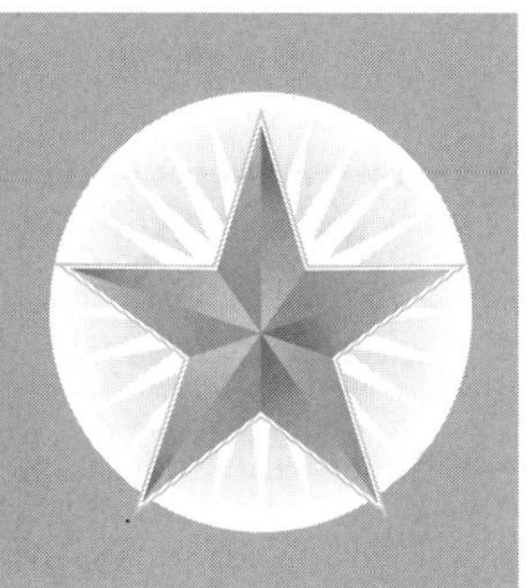

Key Points

- Believe it or not, being a great student is not all about being smart; it's about understanding and making the most of your unique intelligence types. It's about understanding your own strengths and weaknesses. It's about capitalizing on those strengths and working on those weaknesses. And it's about having the right tools and tricks for your particular learning style.

- "Smart" is a misunderstood concept. An IQ is not a complete picture of your abilities. You probably know people who are really book smart, but maybe they have trouble working with people, or they can't get the hang of how to change a tire, or they have almost no creativity.

- People who are book smart have the type of intelligence that works well in the classroom, but there are plenty of other ways to be smart, and the first trick to being a great student is making your intelligence type work for you.

- There are certain traits that all great students share no matter what kind of learners they are. First of all, great students set goals for themselves, goals that guide their decisions about how to spend their time and energy. The best goals are specific—not "I'll do better in school" but "I'll earn at least a 3.5 GPA," for example. They also stretch you a bit; a 3.5 is no big deal if you ended last semester with a 3.4.

- You should try to set at least one goal for yourself in each one of these six areas: academic grades, social life, sports and exercise, family and community, hobbies and interests, and long-term goals. Being happy and healthy is as important as getting good grades.

- Successful students are also organized. They organize their stuff, they organize their time, and they organize their brains. It doesn't mean everything has to be perfectly neat, crisp, and clean. It just means you need to know where to find things quickly. We'll talk about how to do this in a later lecture.

- Great students also lead balanced lives. They realize that success in school is important, but they recognize the importance of friendships, family, and community; extracurricular activities and work; exercise; hobbies—basically, a rich personal life. By extension, outstanding students are also happy. That doesn't mean they're annoyingly, perpetually cheerful; it just means they're fulfilled, meeting goals, and having fun, too.

- Finally, great students are curious. In fact, that's most of what being a student is about. The Zen master Shunryu Suzuki called this having "the beginner's mind," meaning that no matter how good you are at something, you should pretend you're still a beginner. Accept that there's always more to learn. Be curious. Ask questions. Know that you can grow.

The Seven (or So) Types of Intelligence

Howard Gardner is a Harvard-educated developmental psychologist (sounds like a smart guy, right?) who first proposed the theory of multiple intelligences. Gardner described seven different types, and there may be more or fewer depending on how you slice it, but each of us has two or three types of intelligence that can predict our learning style.

- Visual/spatial learners, whom we might call picture smart, love to make art, have vivid imaginations, and think in pictures. They need to see things to understand them; words can sometimes just float on by. In the classroom, they love charts, diagrams, films—anything that puts the idea into pictures. Visual intelligence is one of the most common types.

- Kinesthetic learners have body smarts. They are doers and makers, athletes and builders. They love all sorts of physical activity and anything that keeps their hands busy. Sometimes they find the classroom a little confining; sitting at a desk all day doesn't work well for them. On the other hand, simple physical engagement like taking notes, performing a skit, or building a model can really make things click for these learners.

- Musical learners are all about songs and rhythm. They're often singers and musicians in the literal sense. Good study strategies for this learning type include reading aloud, maybe even singing the information; using mnemonic (memory-related) ditties, like the ABC song we all learned when we were little; listening to instrumental (i.e., jazz, ambient, classical) music while studying; and singing or playing an instrument during study breaks.

Continued from previous page.

- Intrapersonal learners are social beings. They learn by talking and interacting with others. On the down side, they're the type who gets in trouble for talking in class, but on the up side, they love debates and discussions, and they do great with group activities. They're often natural leaders, and they make great tutors, sometimes learning as much by teaching as by being taught.

- Intrapersonal learners are the opposite of interpersonal ones; they like to learn on their own. They are reflective and probably quiet or introverted. They prefer working and studying alone or one-on-one, rather than in a large group. If they are assigned a group project, they perform best on a facet they can work on independently, then merge with others' work. A big advantage for this type is a quiet place to work at home.

- Logical/mathematical learners are one of the two types that do best in a traditional school setting. These are the math whizzes, the organizing gurus, the pattern finders, and the plan makers. Sounds perfect for the classroom, and it is for the most part, but these folks sometimes have trouble with creative tasks or interpersonal skills, which become more and more important after high school.

- Linguistic/verbal learners are the ones with word smarts—the bookworms, brilliant writers, and great speakers. This also works really well in traditional school settings. Like logical learners, they do so well alone that sometimes group work and interpersonal skills get neglected; unlike logical learners, they sometimes struggle in math class—getting bored and distracted, secretly reading a novel under the desk.

Most of us have two or three ways that we learn best; almost no one has only one type of intelligence. Throughout this course, you'll find lots of tips for every type of learner in many different learning situations.

Suggested Reading

Gardner, *Art, Mind, and Brain*.

Tricks to Try

1. On p. 82, you'll find a quick quiz that will help you determine your intelligence type(s). This is one of those times where there are no right or wrong answers. Just be honest. You might learn a lot about yourself.

2. Get a notebook or your digital device of choice and write down your goals. Try to set at least one goal for yourself in each of the six areas mentioned in the lecture: academic grades, social life, sports and exercise, family and community, hobbies and interests, and long-term goals. Once you have them written down, put them where you will see them at least once a day.

Developing Effective Habits in Class

Lecture 2

Topics in This Lecture

- How to organize information for effective learning
- How to prepare for and participate in a class
- How to take notes

Key Points

- From the time you entered school, you've been leaf collecting—that is, picking up pieces of information and, most likely, tossing them into one big pile of "school stuff" in your mind. A great student knows how to organize that information instead, attaching each leaf to a specific branch on his or her knowledge tree.

- At first, the labels on your branches might be as simple as the major subjects in school—math, history, music, whatever. By the time you reach college, those branches will probably have subbranches; for example, science might have different branches for life sciences, physical science, earth science, and so on.

- When a piece of information fits on more than one branch—you might learn fractions in math, then use them in music, chemistry, home, and lots of other places—the best thing to do is to attach the information to all of those branches. Scientists call this multiple encoding; it makes it easier to retrieve the information when you need it.

- Before successful students ever get to class, they've prepared their brains for leaf attachment. They know ahead of time what the next class will be about, either by following an agenda, doing the assigned reading, or just asking the teacher.

- Throughout your school career, you may encounter the same piece of information many times. Don't kid yourself; just because you heard it years ago doesn't mean you know all there is to know on the topic. Keep your mind open, and keep strengthening the connections between leaves and branches. Curiosity is the key to learning.

- Class prep is one of the places you can take advantage of your unique intelligence type. You can make a traditional outline if you're a linguistic/verbal or logical/mathematical learner, or you can start with an actual tree or concept map if you're a visual/spatial learner, and so on.

- Finally, after you create your tree, outline, or other structure that works for you, jot down one simple question that you have about that topic. The idea here is to get your mind asking questions, and not just answering them all of the time.

- To learn, you not only have to prepare; you have to participate. You have to be an active learner. At a minimum this means you have to show up and pay attention. Don't cut class, and don't sit where you'll be easily distracted. Finally, you should be asking questions, either during class or afterward in a one-on-one with your teacher.

- As you learn, your brain is physically building pathways between your brain cells. The more that pathway gets used, the more established it becomes, so make sure your path is going in the right direction before you leave the classroom—a path, once established, is hard to reroute. Practice using your new information and get feedback from your teacher and fellow students on whether or not you've got the concept.

- At this point, a lot of students would be worried that using all these techniques makes them look dorky. First of all, you're not a dork if you're just trying to understand something. Second, if you're worried about how others see you, start small. Ask one question a day. Eventually, you'll be more comfortable asking more questions.

- Unfortunately, not every teacher is assigned to teach what their passion is, and not all teachers have learned how to make learning fun. In those situations, you need to take control of your own education. Meet with your teacher outside class and offer constructive ideas for making class more fun.

- Good note taking is essential, but what's not essential is writing down every tiny detail in a lecture or presentation. Find a system of taking notes that works with your learning style, and always keep it simple. Just jot down the big ideas, and otherwise keep your head up and your attention focused on what's going on.

Trick to Try

1. In the last lecture, you learned how to determine your intelligence type(s). Think about ways to organize information, prepare for class, and participate in class that take advantage of your type:

- If you're a linguistic/verbal learner or logical/mathematical learner, traditional outlining may be the best way for you to build a tree to hang your knowledge on.

- For visual/spatial types, making a concept map or using a visual metaphor might help you organize information.

- Interpersonal and intrapersonal learners can get study buddies or form a study group to prep with.

- Musical and kinesthetic learners, don't be afraid to get out of your chair and get moving. Recite the big concepts, make up tunes about the topic, or associate facts with gestures and movements while prepping—but don't disrupt the classroom by breaking into a song and dance!

Working Cooperatively in Groups

Lecture 3

Topics in This Lecture

- How to structure a group to utilize every member's strengths
- How to communicate tactfully
- How to compromise and reach consensus

Key Points

- Life is a series of group projects. The problem is most of us aren't really all that good them. You have to give up a little piece of yourself to make the group really work. But when groups work, they really work.

- In an effective team, members complement each other's strengths and weaknesses. Everyone is valued for what they can bring to the table, and everyone puts the group's needs ahead of their own.

- In the real world of real people, ideal teams are few and far between. Somebody in the group will be annoying, controlling, lazy, or screwing around. Maybe nobody wants to lead, or maybe too many people want to lead. You—the superstar student—will have to make it work. You'll have to lead.

- Good leaders know what each team member's strengths are, including their own. They know how to divide a big job into several smaller ones and assign them effectively. They also know that a group does not work for the leader; rather, a good leader works for the group.

- The amazing Diamond Geisometer is a tool invented by your humble professor to show how people with different ways of relating to the world—sort of like the different intelligence types—can work together as a group.
    - Factual types are all about the details. They'll nitpick a project—in a good way—and make sure everything is covered.
    - Analytical people are able to take a subject, pick it apart, and get right to the essence of the topic or problem.
    - People who are practical are the ones who get things done. They have street smarts, understand what it will take to finish a task, and can organize everything to make it work.
    - Finally, there are the creative folks. Creativity, in this case, isn't limited to artistic ability, although that could be part of it. It's more like the ability to approach the topic from a unique and exciting point of view.
- What happens when you put all these types together? You end up with group intelligence. You might expect it would be hard for such different people to work together, but it's worth it, because you've filled the diamond.
- If you're working on a long-term group project, it helps to make a table to keep track of vital information. This includes everyone's contact information (and maybe their work, class, or extracurricular schedules); each member's specific assignment; and a deadline for each piece of the project. Make sure everyone has a hard copy and, if possible, access to an electronic copy, too.
- Remember when planning to give yourself some room in the schedule in case someone gets sick, things get lost, or somebody just flakes out. In other words, plan to be finished before the project is due.

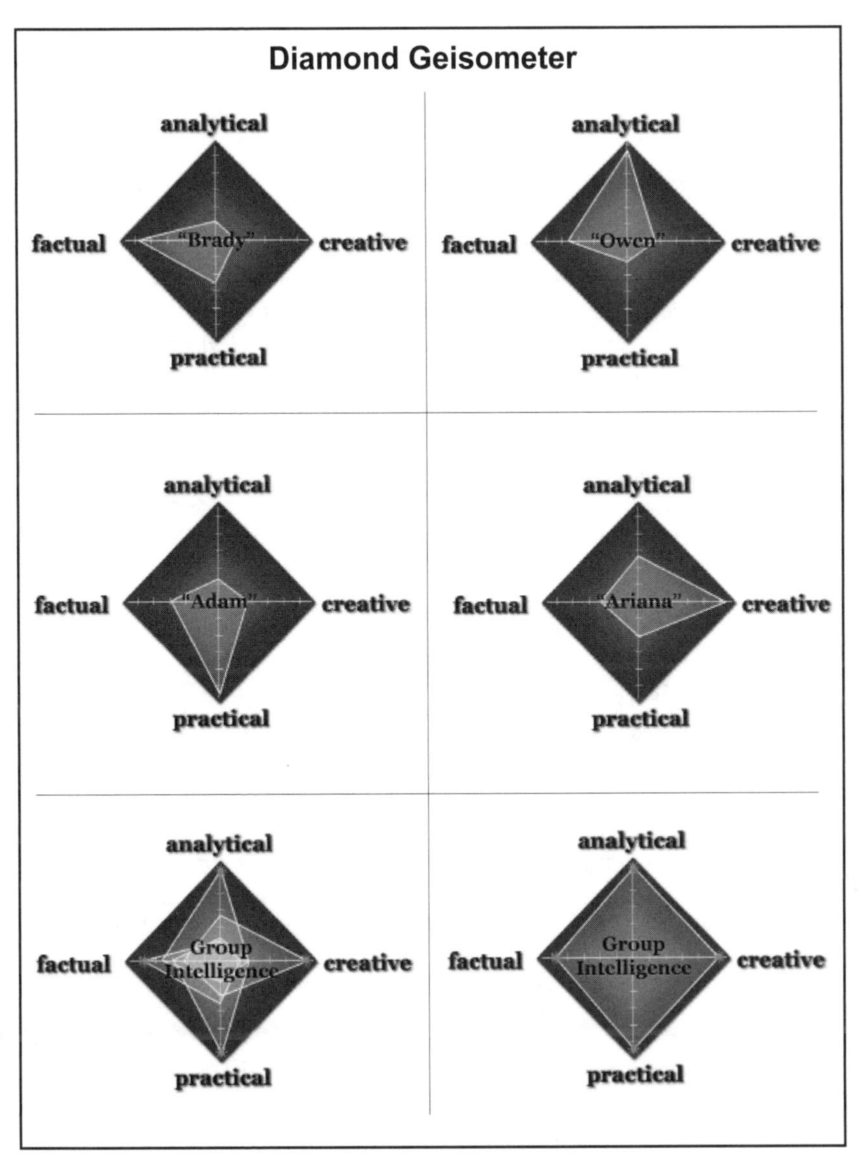

Each of us has different strengths. One way to build an effective group for a school project is to balance the Diamond Geisometer—in other words, make sure your group has at least one member with each intelligence type.

- What do you do when there's a problem or disagreement in your group? You can't get in someone's face, but you can't let someone walk all over the group, either. You need to be able to communicate assertively, but with tact.
    - Being tactful means treating everyone with respect, no matter what your differences, but it also means having a strong commitment to getting the work done.
    - There are lots of verbal strategies for respectful, tactful communication. Use someone's name, not, "Hey, dude." Start with a compliment: "You did an awesome job on *x*, but I'm a little worried about *y*." Soften the language with phrases like "a little." Use the third person to make the comment less personal: "I just want to make sure no one's having trouble hitting the deadline." Finally, offer a specific suggestion to make the situation better: "Hey, I think I have a book with the info you need."
    - Communicating this way might feel a little awkward the first few times try it, but it will get easier with time and eventually become natural.
- One of the biggest mistakes a leader can make is to try to control everyone and everything. A decision based on control or domination is dissatisfying

Example of Weighted Voting

	Paula	Vijay	Samantha	Greg	Total
skit	6	4	1	1	**12**
video	4	1	4	2	**11**
PowerPoint	3	2	5	5	**15**
poster	1	6	3	3	**13**
website	5	3	6	6	**20**
game	2	5	2	4	**13**

In weighted voting, each group member ranks his or her favorite option as 1, second favorite as 2, and so on. The number with the *lowest* score wins. Dot voting is similar, except each member spends *more* of their allotted dots on their preferred option(s), and the option with the highest score wins.

for everyone. It destroys trust, goodwill, and even friendships. Even if one person says "I don't mind," that person probably minds.

- Working toward compromise is better than trying to have your way in everything. Sometimes that means a half-win, half-lose outcome for everyone, but that's better than someone getting a lose-lose. In the best cases, you can find a compromise that's win-win for everyone.

- Good compromise is also about good communication—being honest about your preferences and your reasoning. Once all that is out in the open, you may be able to put matters to a straight-up vote. If more than two options are in play, dot voting and weighted voting, where people rank their preferences among the options, are good alternatives. More informally, you can use "I can live with these" voting or an "I narrow, you choose" system.

Suggested Reading

Goleman, *Emotional Intelligence.*

———, *Social Intelligence.*

Tricks to Try

1. Look for examples of tactful (and not-so-tactful) talk in your everyday life—in online forums, between family members, between politicians, among reality show cast mates, and so on. Once you think you've got the pattern down, start practicing tactful talk yourself. Just imagine how much better it might work than the old standbys "Mom and Dad, can I *pleeeeeeeeease* … ?" and "But it's not fair!"

2. Compromising on a project when your grades are on the line can be a tense situation, to say the least. The next time you and your friends have to make a more casual decision—which movie to see, where to get lunch, or something like that—give one of the systems described in this lecture a try. Getting used to compromise when the stakes are low makes it feel more natural when the stakes are high.

Managing Time and Organizing Spaces

Lecture 4

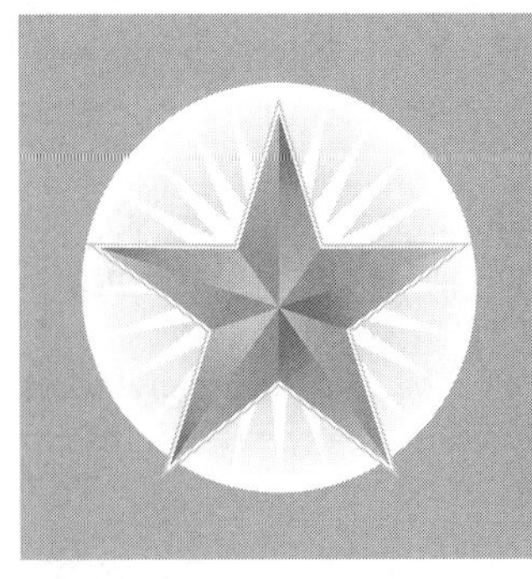

Topics in This Lecture

- The myth of multitasking
- Making a weekly plan
- Organized spaces

Key Points

- It's time to learn how to manage time—how to prioritize tasks, schedule your time efficiently, and get your stuff organized. Not only will you navigate your busy life more effectively when you're organized; you'll end up with more free time to do those things you really like to do.

- When you're a teen, your brain is growing and building neural pathways faster than at almost any other time in your life. It's like a sleek, sexy sports car capable of mind-blowing speed … with lousy handling. In other words, while your capacity to learn is at its max, your planning, prioritizing, and self-control haven't quite caught up.

- While you, like most people you know, probably feel you have too much to do and too little time, you actually have more time than you think. Most teens spend about 40 percent of their time asleep and another 10 percent in school. Fully 50 percent of your time is available for everything from homework to hanging out. So how do you make the most of this time?

- First, let's dismiss the myth of multitasking. Yes, all of us do it. No, none of us are good at it. Not even teens. Not even *you*. All scientific data—both psychological and neurological data on people in every age group—indicate that there is no such thing as multitasking. We're actually just switching our attention among tasks.

- The result of this task switching is twofold: One, no one task is getting the full attention it needs to be done well, and two, believe it or not, the "better" you are at multitasking (that is, the more things you *think* you can do at once), the worse you are at everything you're doing. Dramatically worse—studies say about 40 percent worse. If that's not bad enough, multitasking is just plain rude to people you're trying to interact with at the time. It makes you a jerk.

- So if multitasking is pretty useless, why do we do it? The answer lies on the prehistoric savannah. Our brains evolved to notice and react to little changes in our environment. "Bing! You've got mail," is a lot less urgent than "Bing! You're about to be eaten," but our brains respond the same way and even reward us with positive vibes (or rather, neurochemicals) for noticing. The only way to stop the response is to eliminate the distractions from your environment.

- At the outset, we mentioned that teens aren't the greatest at planning ahead. This is where good organization can really help you, and organization starts with setting weekly goals. At the end of this lecture guide, you'll find a sample weekly goals list and a simple system for organizing them. Try out that exercise, then try it with your own goals.

- Personal scheduling, just like group work scheduling, should have a built in cushion whenever possible. Emergencies will come up now and again. So if you've got time to write that paper ahead of time, if you've got a few weeks warning for that midterm, if you've got a few months before you go off book for the school play, plan to get your writing, studying, and memorizing done before they're due. That way, if disaster strikes, you'll still be on time.

- Lots of good, inexpensive tools exist for helping you plan. They can be as simple as multiple colors of sticky notes and an empty stretch of wall to paper calendars to free or cheap apps for your phone. But whatever you use, the basic process is to prioritize your goals, putting what you have to do ahead of what you only want to do and organizing them according to when you need them done.

- When you're done organizing your time, you need to organize your paperwork (or your computer desktop, online file storage, or whatever you use). All papers—literal or virtual—should go into folders, labeled or color-coded according to subject or activity. Remember that pocket folders have two sides and use that to your advantage: "To Do" and "Done," "Due Soon" and "Due Later," or something similar. For long-

Making Time for Time Out

You have to give up multitasking to be a superstar student—no exceptions. But that's not saying you have to give up television, texting, or any of your favorite stress-relieving, social life–enhancing stuff. The key is time management.

- Set aside 20- or 30-minute chunks of time to study or do homework with no interruptions—none. Turn off your phone and televison; log out of Facebook, chat, and e-mail. Kick out your friends and siblings. Focus every ounce of attention you've got on the task at hand.

- After each intense work session, take a break. Check your phone and e-mail, grab a snack, go for a run, whatever … then shut it all off and start over. Do this as many times as it takes to get through your workload for the day.

With a system like this, not only will the quality of your work improve, but you'll get it done faster and have more time left over for fun.

term storage, pull papers from working folders and stick them in a box or file drawer dedicated to the term. You may need to find them later.

- In general, the simplest systems work the best for most people; the more complex and time-consuming they are to maintain, the more likely you are to give up on them. Keep in mind, though, your system only has to work for one person: you. Don't worry if it looks messy or confusing to others, as long as it works for you.

Suggested Reading

Rosen, "The Myth of Multitasking."

Trick to Try

Let's practice weekly planning using sticky notes. I recommend color coding either the notes themselves or the ink you use on them; if you're color blind, try using different sizes or shapes for your notes instead.

Here's your imaginary to do list for the week:

Task	Notes
basketball practice	every day after school until 5 p.m. (except Tues.)
basketball game	Tues. 5:00–8:30 p.m.
math worksheets	about 30 minutes each, 1 due Weds. and 1 due Fri.
research paper	about 3 hours left, due Fri.
science lab write-up	about 1 hour, due Tues.
Spanish vocab/practice	every weeknight, 20 minutes
geography midterm	study for 2+ hours, test on Thurs.
science test	study for 1 hour, test on Fri.
youth group	Weds. 6:00–7:30 p.m.
visit uncle in hospital	any evening, 1 hour

favorite TV shows	Tues. and Thurs., 8–9 p.m.
work	Sat., 8 a.m.–4 p.m.
go to movies with friends	any evening or weekend, 3 hours
volunteer at shelter	any day/time before 9 p.m.
household chores	as needed throughout week, 1–2 hours total

1. Label one set of sticky notes with the days of the week and stick them along your blank wall. You may want to run labels vertically for morning/afternoon/evening or before school/after school/after dinner too, or you can just remember that higher means earlier and lower means later.

2. Prioritize the items in this list. Put all the items that have a fixed date and time on one color note and all the flexible items on a different color.

3. Take the fixed items and start scheduling them in by sticking them to the appropriate spot on the wall. Remember to build in a cushion for papers and exams whenever possible.

4. Once you're satisfied with where the fixed items are, start slotting in the flexible ones.

5. Don't forget to leave time for sleeping, eating, showering, and all that!

All done? Great. Now take a step back and survey your work. It's a big list; were you surprised at how easy it was to find time for everything or by how much time you've got left over? Did you find yourself struggling to prioritize school and work over fun, or did the balance seem pretty fair? Are you confident that in an emergency you could shift things around and still meet your goals?

As with anything else in life, practice makes … well, maybe not perfect, but hopefully painless. Take a few minutes now (or at least before you start the next lecture) to write up a list of your own weekly tasks and play around with this system or another one that you think would work better for you.

Taking Charge of Homework

Lecture 5

Topics in This Lecture

- Creating good study environments
- Study techniques for different intelligences
- How to take notes

Key Points

- What's the point of homework? In a word: practice. Just like practicing free throws or guitar licks or driving, homework helps you embed the knowledge and perfect the skills you need to succeed. You're paving your neural pathways so they become highways.

- Not all homework is just a repeat of what you've already done in class; a good teacher will give assignments that connect your classroom knowledge to the real world or make you use your knowledge in a new and challenging way. Good homework can be engaging and even fun.

- It's your right as a student to have meaningful homework. If you feel like your teacher is assigning drudgery and busy work, it's okay to talk with him or her about it—respectfully and tactfully, just the way you learned to approach your peers. Suggest some ways to make your homework more relevant or fun.

- When it comes to studying, you've probably been told to pick a comfortable, quiet place and stick with it. Brain research, however, says just the opposite. Studying the same concept in multiple locations creates more associations in your brain and helps you retain and retrieve concepts better. But that doesn't mean studying just anywhere. You still need a distraction-free zone, and you need a place where all the materials you need are close at hand.

© Digital Vision/Thinkstock.

No matter what type of learner you are, you should study in a place with no distractions.

- One of the dangers of taking study breaks is checking your e-mail or phone and suddenly getting sucked into the drama going on outside your study spot. Sometimes you're going to have to be firm with friends who want more than a quick text. If they're true friends and they know your goals, they'll support you. You might just inspire them, too.

- Physical exercise is good for your brain. Blood pumping through your circulatory system brings your brain the fuel it needs and removes waste products. If you're starting to get sleepy while you're reading, get up and move around, either while reading or during a break.

- Different intelligence types need different kinds of study environments and techniques, but the key for every type is not to read passively; just attacking the text with a highlighter isn't enough for most of us, either. You need to interact with the material in the way or ways best suited to your brain. A number of techniques are listed in the Tricks to Try on p. 24–25. It's worth experimenting and keeping track of what works for you and what doesn't.

- Every type of learner needs to take notes of some sort, so it's important to do it well. Let's look at three different ways to pull the main ideas from any article, book, website, or other written material. One of these, or a variation on one, should work for just about everybody. Each starts with asking questions about the material before you read it:

- Why am I reading this? Core material will need intense attention to every word; in supplemental material, some sections can be skimmed while you focus on others.

- What's the big picture? The title may or may not be a dead giveaway here; look at the intro and conclusion, too.

- What are the important points? Generally, 80 percent of the important information is found within 20 percent of the text. Looking at headings, images, and so forth will help you figure out which 20 percent to focus on.

- Now the big question: How can I organize the main points in a way that works for me? The big three methods are traditional outlining, mind mapping, and annotating.

  - Traditional outlining is pulling the skeleton out of the text. The main headings will give you the top-level outline points,

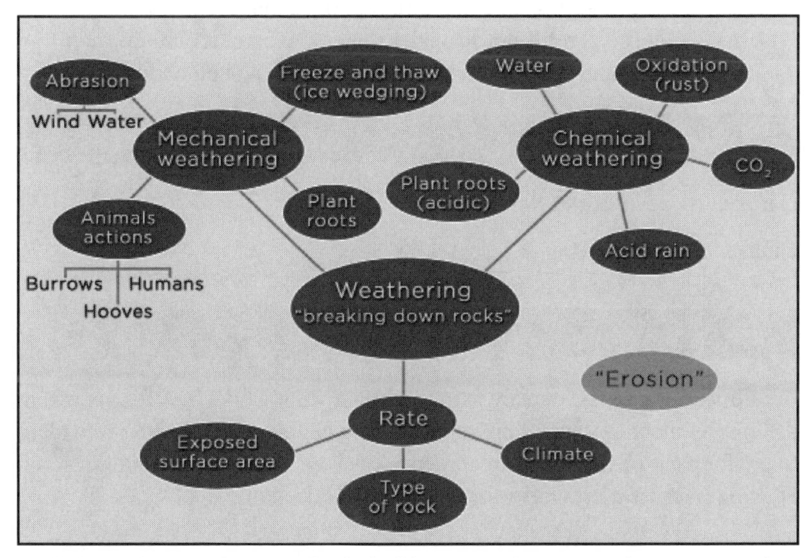

A mind map is a nonlinear method of taking notes that uses colors, arrows, size, and other visual cues to record information, rather than just words.

subheadings will give you the second-level points, and any lower-level points will be found in the main body of the text. You should be able to pick them out pretty easily when you know the main points they're meant to support.

- Mind mapping, or concept mapping, is more illustrative and good for visual learners in particular. The title or main topic of the text goes in the middle of the page, and the main points radiate out from it. Lower-level points radiate off the main points. You can even make cross-connections among points. Use different ink colors, different bubble and arrow shapes, and so on to make relationships stand out. Be careful, though. It's possible to go overboard and create an unreadable mess.

- Annotating text means marking up in the text and writing in its margins. Important points are underlined or highlighted. In the margins, you try to summarize the point of a section in your own words. If you can re-explain an idea, you've probably got a good grasp on it. Again, color coding helps, and you have to be careful not to make a mess. Whatever you do, don't go annotating someone else's book! Make a photocopy to work on.

Suggested Reading

Gardner, *Art, Mind, and Brain.*

Gelb, *Think like Da Vinci.*

Tricks to Try

For all learning types, the key is to figure out what works best for you, from the environment to scheduling to note-taking technique. Here are some ideas to try for each of Gardner's intelligence types. It's worth experimenting and keeping track of what works for you and what doesn't.

Intelligence Type	Study Strategies
Visual learners	Mind mapping Posting important points and images on the walls of your study area Making drawings (literal or metaphorical) of key concepts Keeping your study area bare and well-organized to minimize visual distractions
Kinesthetic learners	Typing out your notes as you read Walking while reading (watch out for obstacles!) Keeping your hands busy with a stress ball, yo-yo, or other small object as you read
Musical learners	Reading your notes into a digital recorder and playing them back as you drive or work out Explaining concepts aloud among study buddies Creating mnemonic rhymes and songs
Interpersonal learners	Studying with people around (at the kitchen table, in a coffee shop, in the school library) Taking social breaks between each study session or topic (If you can, review the material with a friend or family member during the break) Taking on group projects and interview projects when available
Intrapersonal learners	Having a quiet, cozy workspace Keeping separate, attractive journals for each subject
Logical learners	Mixing up study locations and styles (i.e., alone versus in groups) Making charts and graphs Reverse engineering an outline from a text
Linguistic learners	Read alone, but review with a partner or group Create flash cards Write mnemonics

Developing a Creative Mind

Lecture 6

Topics in This Lecture

- Mind-sets you need to think creatively
- Practical techniques for getting creative
- Why creativity is important in school and in life

Key Points

- Lots of people don't get the difference between artistic ability and creativity. Creativity is much broader than being able to play an instrument or paint a picture. Simply defined, it is the ability to come up with something new (new to you or new to the whole world) that has a value or utility. Creativity can happen anywhere, in any field, at any time.

- To create something truly new, we sometimes have to bend or break the rules—and a lot of the time, these rules aren't rules at all but just "the way we've always done it." We just assume that we can't change or challenge anything.

- One of the easiest ways to "break" the rules at school in a good way is to talk to your teacher about alternative assignments, projects outside the scope of the regularly assigned homework. Most teachers love it when students show this kind of creativity and initiative.

- Using a bit of creativity in school—how you study, how you do projects, and how you ask questions—makes it more fun to learn, it makes information stick better in your brain, and makes you a more interesting, well-rounded person.

- Traditionally, our educational system has valued structure over creativity. Parents and teachers alike expect you to become more mature and responsible—both great things!—but often at the expense of curiosity, creativity, and play.

- You may think you're not the creative type, but creativity is a skill that can be developed. You were born thinking creatively, so the key to rediscovering your buried creativity is to be more childlike (which is not the same as being immature!). You need to approach learning as if it's a game or an adventure. Relax, let your mind fill with possibilities, and don't worry about winning or losing, being judged or being graded.

- Maybe you've tried a trick that your teacher might call free writing and that your friends probably call puking on the page—just writing down anything and everything that comes into your head, whether or not it's useful or relevant or important. Typically, you find there's at least one idea on that page that's worth exploring. Coming up with possibilities in this way is called divergent thinking.

- After you do this kind of filter-free brainstorming, then you can move on to step two, convergent

The Three Rules of Brainstorming

1. Brainstorm by yourself, and then combine your ideas with others' later. Research shows that you will get more ideas that way.

2. There are no bad ideas when brainstorming. Don't evaluate; just create.

3. There are no good ideas when brainstorming. If you edit and criticize too early, you won't come up with anything useful.

thinking, which means evaluating and refining the ideas you've just produced into something workable.

- Another mind-set creative people share is the willingness to fail. Failure is not only an option; it's an essential part of the creative process. It means you're taking risks, and without risk taking, you'll never come up with anything new.

- It's easier to take risks if you know you have the support of your friends, family, and teachers. Getting that support means communicating well with these folks, and communicating well means having strong, honest relationships with them. This is why family and friends should be part of your goal-setting process. We all need these relationships to thrive and succeed.

© iStockphoto/Thinkstock.

If sitting at the desk stifles your creativity, get up, get out, get moving!

- Word association is a great technique for brainstorming. If your brain blanks out on you, try choosing a random set of words from the dictionary or other book and try to relate them to your topic. Forcing unrelated words into analogies, no matter how bizarre, can produce interesting and inspiring results. Most creative art—whether visual, written, or performed—is based on making connections between two or more things that don't naturally go together.

- Sitting at the same desk at the same time every day can stifle your creativity. A change of scene can help when you're stuck. Going for a walk or a run can also free your creative brain up to do better thinking. Even just following web links at random can open up new possibilities. Reading a book or article you would never usually read, talking to people you don't usually talk to, trying to see the world through someone (or something) else's perspective are all ways to jump-start your idea machine.

- Why is creativity so important? It will keep you from becoming obsolete in the global economy, because you'll be better able to meet new challenges. Most of the problems the world faces today can't be solved with the same kinds of thinking that was used in the past. Creativity also makes you a more interesting person, not to mention a more interested and engaged one.

Suggested Reading

Clegg and Birch, *Instant Creativity*.

Robinson, *Out of Our Minds*.

Tricks to Try

1. Is word association not working for you? Try word disassociation. Get together with a friend or two and try coming up with a series of words that have *nothing* to do with each other. It's harder than it sounds, and it can make for some interesting connections, because you'll discover relationships between ideas you thought were entirely separate.

2. If your brain's freezing up when you think about your assigned topic and you've tried all the ideas mentioned in the lecture, ask your teacher if it's all right for you and a friend to brainstorm for each other's topics, then give each other your lists of ideas. Taking the immediate pressure off in this way might relax you enough to let your mind play.

Thinking Critically

Lecture 7

Topics in This Lecture

- The role of evidence in critical thinking
- The role of emotions in critical thinking
- The role of logic in critical thinking

Key Points

- Creative and critical thinking go hand in hand. It's great to be open to new ideas, but to make use of them you have to determine which ideas are the best and what to do with them. Critical thinking is the process of evaluating the evidence supporting an idea by using logic and reason, rather than emotion, gut instinct, or intuition.

- Critical thinking is hard work. It's also the difference between a good student and a great student. It's an essential skill you will use throughout your life to make the best decisions about what to believe and how to act.

- Critical thinking is the opposite of blind acceptance. Blind acceptance means considering just one idea and sticking with it. It's the opposite of the creative thinking–critical thinking cycle. Critical thinkers also aren't afraid to change their views when new, better evidence comes along.

- Whether you're writing a research paper, drawing conclusions about a science experiment, or trying to persuade people to change their behaviors, you have to have evidence to support your claims. Evidence can range from simple personal observations to a huge scientific study.

But not all evidence is equally valid. The best evidence is relevant, balanced, and fits with the other pieces of evidence you have.

- When evaluating evidence, you need to be aware of common logical fallacies. Two of the most common are (1) confusing correlation with causation and (2) making sweeping generalizations.

    - When we say that correlation does not imply causation, we mean that just because two things appear together, we can't be sure one caused the other. Did studying help you pass the test? Almost certainly. Did wearing your lucky socks help you pass the test? Probably not. The difference is that we know the mechanism connecting studying and good grades; a mechanism linking grades to hosiery has never been demonstrated.

    - Sweeping generalizations are conclusions built on too little or very weak evidence. The most common cause of this is the anecdote: "I once met a rich person who was a snob; therefore, all rich people are snobs." Don't grab the first evidence you find and think that it's enough to confirm your opinion—or build a research paper on. The bigger your pool of evidence, the more likely you are to draw a correct conclusion.

- One of the biggest challenges in good critical thinking is making sure you are looking at balanced evidence. In a courtroom, a judge hears testimony and arguments from both sides of the case. In the same way, you need to consider multiple points of view before coming to a conclusion. Always consider what bias or agenda your source might have, whether that source is a person or an organization.

- One great trick for strengthening your own arguments is to argue against them. Pretend you disagree with your own position; how would you go about countering the argument? Where are the weak points?

Logical Fallacies and Appeals to Emotion

Lots of arguments are built on the shaky ground of strong emotion and poor logic. Here's a list of problems to watch out for in your arguments and the arguments of others:

Ad hominem: Attacking a person rather than the evidence to discredit the person's opinion. "Are you going to take car-buying advice from someone who hates pizza?"

Appeal to authority: Accepting the opinion of someone powerful, regardless of the quality of his or her supporting evidence. This is a particular problem when an authority in one area gives an opinion in on a topic outside his or her area of expertise.

Appeal to common belief: Accepting an opinion or belief as correct just because a large number of people hold it. Also known as the bandwagon effect.

Appeal to fear: Using worst-case scenarios and other negative images to frighten a person into believing an argument, despite the statistical likelihood (or unlikelihood) of a bad outcome.

Appeal to pity: Acting in someone's short-term favor because that person has suffered, not because it's the best for that person in the long term or best for everyone.

Begging the question: An argument that rests on evidence that itself needs to be proven. "This is the best movie of the year because it made the most money" assumes that profitability is evidence of quality.

Circular reasoning: An argument where the premise and the conclusion are almost identical. "I'm the best teacher in the world because I'm a better teacher than everyone else."

Continued from previous page.

False dilemma: Turning a complex situation into a black-and-white one. "If Mom and Dad don't buy me a car for graduation, it proves they don't love me." There are a lot of reasons why you got that laptop instead.

Linear thinking: Turning a complicated web of causes and effects into a chain of events or reasons.

Slippery slope: Claiming that one action, particularly one misstep or failure, will cause an chain reaction of undesirable events. "If you fail this vocabulary test you'll ruin your entire high school career and end up unemployed."

Straw man: Exaggerating the features of your opponent's argument to make it seem outrageous or ridiculous. "My opponent wants a one percent cut in military funding. He wants us to be defenseless against terrorism!"

Style over substance: Being swayed by how evidence is presented, rather than by the quality of the evidence. For example, people are more likely to trust the opinions of people they find attractive or people they already know and like.

- Another technique is to write your main points and then write the evidence for each point beneath it. Seeing it all laid out may show you that you're short on evidence for one of your claims or that the evidence itself is weak or biased.

- Emotions are a good thing, but we shouldn't make our decisions based only on emotion. You need to evaluate ideas based on their own merits, not on how you feel about them. Check the box above for a list of common ways emotions trip up our analyses.

- The role of logic in making an argument is to build a solid case using a good line of reasoning or to find flaws in someone else's case by using good reasoning. The sidebar also contains a list of common logical fallacies—arguments that sound like good lines of reasoning but aren't. Knowing how to identify bad logic will help you to avoid using it in your own arguments.

- The world is a more complex place than we'd like to admit. There usually aren't straightforward answers or simple solutions to real-world problems. The point of critical thinking is to recognize and to explore the complexity of the world instead of trying to oversimplify it and make it linear.

Suggested Reading

Baggini and Fosl, *The Philosopher's Toolkit.*

McInerny, *Being Logical.*

Tricks to Try

1. The next time you're watching television, watch the commercials with a critical eye and ask yourself what the advertisers are trying to get you to believe about their product. How much of what you're seeing and hearing has to do with what the product actually does, and how much of it is about making you feel something about the product?

2. One useful tool for making real-world decisions is to build a decision matrix. Pretend you're looking to buy a car. Make a table that lists all the cars you would like to have along one axis and all the features you need or want along the other. Next, figure out which of the features are most important; for example, do you need lots of room to haul stuff around, or is good gas mileage more important? Like the weighted voting we did in Lecture 3, give each car one point for having "want" features and two, three, or more points for having "need" features. When you add up the points, does the best choice become pretty clear?

Diving into Research

Lecture 8

Topics in This Lecture

- Preparing to do research
- Searching for information
- Evaluating your sources
- Organizing your information

Key Points

- Effective, efficient research is a huge factor in the success of any student and in life. Because there is so much information out there, it's harder than ever to find the good stuff, evaluate it accurately, and use it effectively. This is where the critical thinking skills addressed in Lecture 7 come in.

- Before you dive into research, you need to decide where to dive, how deep to dive, and why you're diving in the first place. Different types of project require different amounts of detail and supporting research. Different goals will mean different strategies—are you writing to inform, to persuade, or for some other purpose?

- All research starts with general sources, such a textbook, an encyclopedia, or a website. When you find something within the general subject that piques your interest, you can start to develop a thesis—the statement you are going to try to support or prove.

- A good thesis is not just a topic; it's a point of view. For example, if your topic is Japanese-American internment camps during World War II, your thesis might be whether or not they were justified. Because a thesis is essentially an opinion, don't be surprised if your opinion evolves, or even reverses, as your research progresses.

- Once you've formed a thesis, it's a good idea to run it by your teacher. He or she can help you shape your basic ideas, give you some ideas about where to look for further information, and even help you avoid dead ends.

- To move from general sources to specific ones, one of the best places to start is the bibliography of your general source or sources. There you'll find books on specific topics, as well as names of prominent experts who may have written other books or articles.

- When your topic is time-sensitive, you'll need to rely less on books and more on peer-reviewed, scholarly journals. These can be harder to find than other sources. You can search for them using the Scholar option on Google, where you can usually read the article's abstract (or summary) to make sure it's relevant. But you may only be able to get the full text via a library.

- If you're having trouble finding answers, don't hesitate to contact experts by phone or e-mail. Be concise and specific with your questions and respectful of their time; odds are they'll be happy to share their wisdom.

- The further you get in school, the more rigorous your research needs to be, and the more scrupulously you must evaluate your sources. Review them carefully for logical fallacies, emotional appeals, ratio of hard data to anecdotes, the author's credentials, the publisher's reputation, and any potential bias involved.

- The more advanced the class, the more likely you'll need to use a combination of primary and secondary sources. Primary sources are original, firsthand data: the Declaration of Independence, original laboratory experiment results, video of a historic event, and so forth. Secondary sources are someone's interpretation or analysis of primary sources, such as your textbook or a modern historian's book about the Declaration.

Reviewing Your Research—SHLAO

Here's an easy to remember, five-step process for getting the best information out of your sources called SHLAO:

- **S stands for skim**. Skim through the text to pick out where the information you need is found.
- **H stands for hard copy**. Make a physical copy of the text—a photocopy, a printout, whatever—that you can mess with until your heart's content.
- **L stands for label**. Label the hard copy with the information you'll need for your bibliography—usually the author, title, publisher, publishing date, and so on. (Ask your teacher or check your assignment for the correct format.) You should also keep a running digital copy of your bibiliography as you work so you can easily add, delete, edit, and finally print and submit it.
- **A stands for annotate**. Mark that baby up! Use one of the techniques described in Lecture 5 for making notes on your reading.
- **O stands for organize**. Use different colored highlighters to mark pro and con arguments, staple or file related texts together, pin information to a cork board in the order you want to use it … whatever helps you find the information quickly when you need it.

- When evaluating the quality of a website, check the domain name first. Remember that .com websites are commercial—anyone can put one up. The .gov domain is reserved for the U.S. government, and other nations have similar domains. An .edu (or in Britain, an .ac.uk) is usually a school or university; a .org is a nonprofit organization. Each of these gives you a clue as to the quality of the information.

- How do you know if you have enough research to get started? It depends on the project, but you should at a minimum understand the main arguments for and against your thesis and have a good balance of "soft" and "hard" evidence—personal or anecdotal evidence and hard information like quotes and statistics.

Tricks to Try

1. Set aside some free time—maybe even use one of your study breaks—to play with the advanced search options on your favorite browser. Pick a fun subject like your favorite band or television show and see what kind of information turns up with different search terms.

2. Contacting experts for your research projects requires the same sort of respect and tact we discussed in group work and working with your teacher. If you're not sure about your pitch, have a parent or teacher review the e-mail you plan to send, or have them role play the phone conversation with you.

Writing Well

Lecture 9

Topics in This Lecture

- The power of words and sentences
- Building paragraphs
- Organizing essays
- Drafting and editing

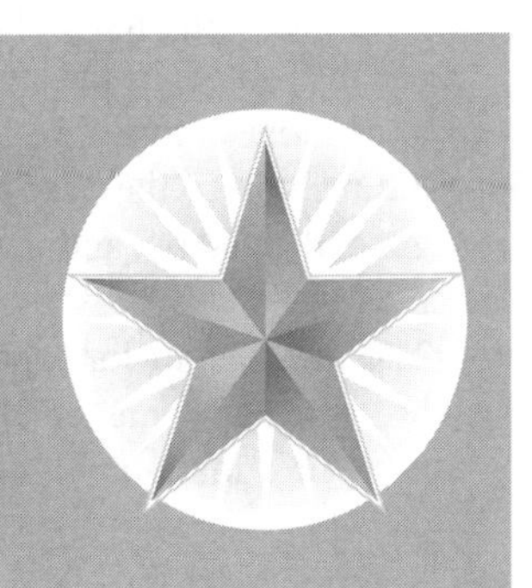

Key Points

- Good writing is simply writing that accurately reflects what you're trying to say, no more, no less. No matter what learning styles you have, you can master writing by understanding the power of word choice and the power of structure.

- Words not only have literal meanings; they also have emotional effects on the reader. Words like "war," "secret," "love," "home," and "prickle" evoke moods, memories, and physical sensations. Thus, choosing the right word can increase the impact of your argument on the reader.

- As with many things, less is more when it comes to high-impact vocabulary. Use strong words strategically to make them stand out. Good writers learn to use words well by observation—that is, reading. They also learn by practice—writing and letting others read their writing.

- Imagine a human body with no skeleton—a blob of goo unable to function. An essay with no structure is the same thing; it's a pile of facts and anecdotes with no meaning. The order and organization of your sentences and paragraphs makes an enormous difference in how well you get your point across.

- A typical paragraph contains one main idea about one topic. Everything in that paragraph should relate to that one main idea. The main idea is usually stated in the first sentence. Supporting details, examples, and arguments follow. The last sentence makes a concluding statement and a transition to the next topic. Think of it as having an hourglass shape: general, specific, and general again.

- The best length for a paragraph really depends on the paragraph. One test is to ask someone else to read your draft and mark where they want more information or where they got confused by too much data.

- In its simplest form, an essay has three parts: a beginning, a middle, and an end. You can think of these three parts as "I tell you what I'm going to tell you," "I tell you," and "I tell you what I told you." A classic five-paragraph essay, for example, has an introduction, three main points, and a conclusion.

- The introductory paragraph is a condensed version of the whole paper. Often, it starts with a story or a broad statement that captures the reader's interest, then states the paper's thesis or argument. The body of the essay is where to expand, develop, and support your thesis. Three paragraphs is usually a minimum, but use as many as it takes to make your point. The conclusion has the opposite shape of the introductory paragraph: from specific to general. Restating your thesis in different words and expanding it by suggesting further research, making parallels with other situations, or applying your topic to the larger world.

- It's good to include some opposing arguments in the body of the paper, but don't build straw man arguments so you can tear them down easily. Present a solid, honest argument from the other side, and then dispute it with evidence and data.

- In what order should you make your points? Chronological events should be presented chronologically; otherwise, it's best to move from

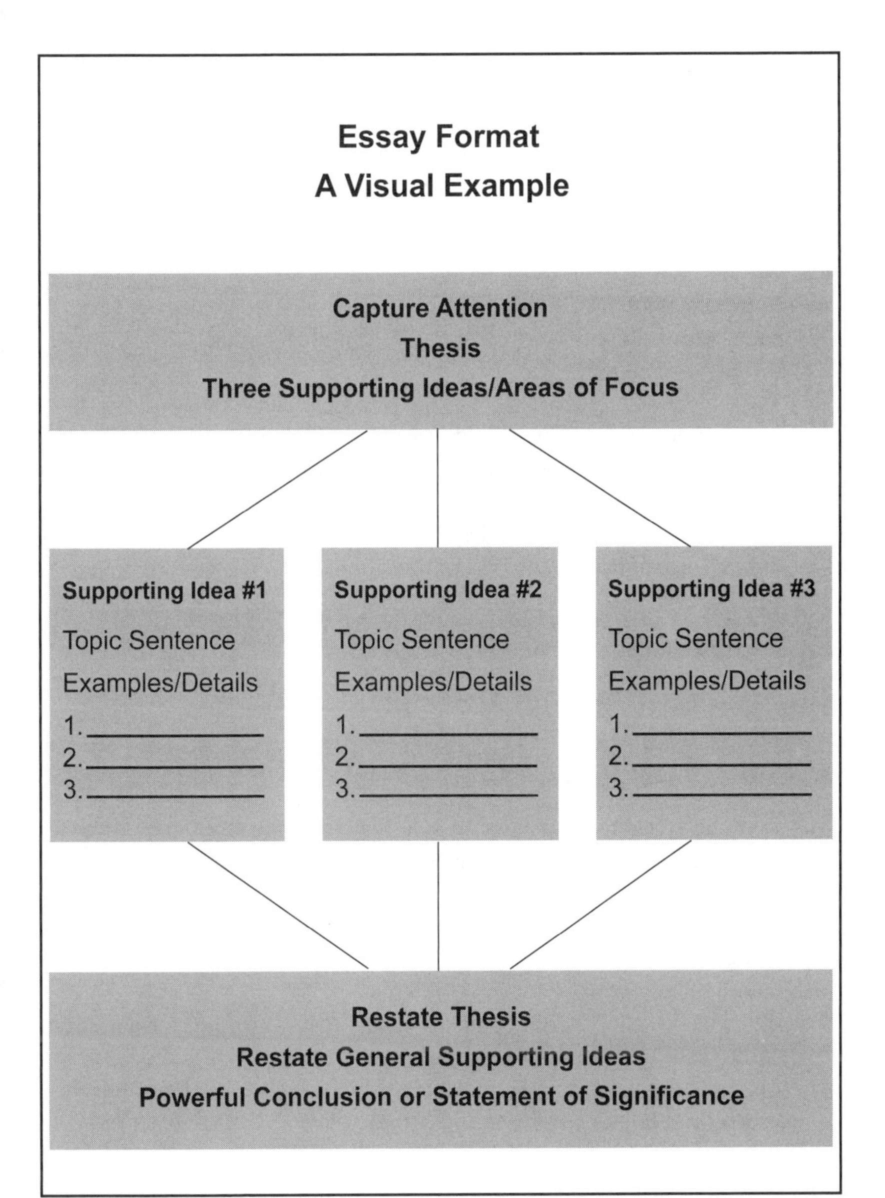
Essay Format
A Visual Example
Capture Attention
Thesis
Three Supporting Ideas/Areas of Focus
Supporting Idea #1
Topic Sentence
Examples/Details
1.
2.
3.
Supporting Idea #2
Topic Sentence
Examples/Details
1.
2.
3.
Supporting Idea #3
Topic Sentence
Examples/Details
1.
2.
3.
Restate Thesis
Restate General Supporting Ideas
Powerful Conclusion or Statement of Significance

your weakest point to your strongest—after all, the last thing you say is most likely to be remembered.

- When your assignment is 15 pages instead of 5 paragraphs, the same principles apply, but the sections get longer. Whatever you do, don't think your teacher will be fooled by bigger margins and larger fonts.

- Your first draft should be just that—a draft. Get your ideas down and don't worry about making it pretty. Let it sit for a day, then do your revising and editing.

- Revise your essay in two or three separate steps. First, read through for the overall ideas, the arguments, the evidence, and the flow. On your second pass, look for word choice, spelling errors, and grammar/ punctuation mistakes. If you have time for a third read-through, look for places you can make better use of transitions.

Suggested Reading

McDonald, *Writing, the Bridge Between Us*.

Tricks to Try

1. Take the lyrics to your favorite song or a passage from your favorite book and analyze the words the author used for their emotional impact as well as their literal meaning. Then play around with them a bit and see what happens. See if you can make a sad song funny, a comic dialogue dramatic, and so forth.

2. If you have a study partner or study group, make the time to swap essay drafts before you revise them. Early readers can give you feedback on what's strong, what's weak, what confusing, what needs more evidence, which dead horses you're beating. If you have a writing center at your school, take advantage of it.

Delivering Dynamic Presentations

Lecture 10

Topics in This Lecture

- Preparing presentations intelligently
- Practicing good delivery
- Effective presentation visuals

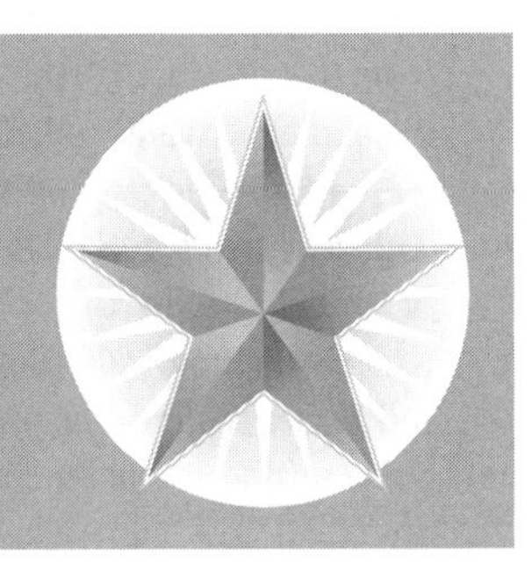

Key Points

- When making a speech, you have about a minute to convince your audience that you're worth listening to. That's why, just as with an essay, you need to start a speech or presentation with a hook. Stories, surprising facts, and powerful or funny images make great hooks. Once you have them hooked, state your thesis.

- Many people fear public speaking, and they've gotten silly and mostly useless advice like picturing your audience wearing only black socks. Thorough preparation and practice is a much better strategy.

- The parts of a speech are a lot like the parts of an essay: introduction, supporting details, and conclusion. But for most of us, simply writing a paper and reading it aloud is a bad strategy. You will sound stiff, stilted, and unnatural. You'll be interacting with a piece of paper instead of with your audience.

- Figure out your main points before you write an introduction or thesis. It can be hard to state what you're going to talk about before you know what you're going to talk about!

- Good preparation starts with a good topic. If you have a choice of topics, choose something with these three characteristics: it's something you know about, something you love to talk about, and something the audience wants to hear about.

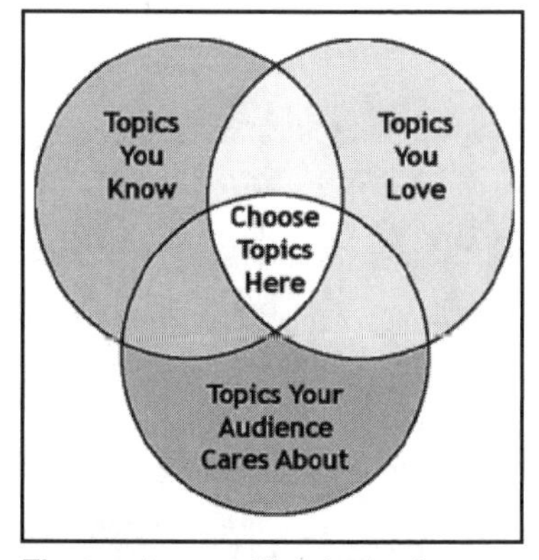

The most compelling topics for presentations are found where knowledge and passion meet.

- The next step is to create an outline or concept map of your speech. Keep your notes simple. The only full sentences in your notes should be your thesis statement and any direct quotes. Otherwise, use key words or phrases, and be ready to speak about them off the cuff at presentation time. (That said, if you're a drama club type with experience memorizing lines and repeating them in interesting ways, writing out your speech and memorizing it may be a good technique for you.)

- Once you have your notes, practice practice practice! Present to your friends, your family members, your dog, anyone. The more you tread those neural pathways, the more relaxed you'll be at presentation time.

- Don't limit your practice sessions to the words you're going to use. You should also be practicing your technique.

    - Keep your head up and make eye contact with the audience members. Only take quick glances at your notes to keep yourself on track.

    - Make sure to address more than one audience member. Don't just stare at your teacher or your best friend the whole time. Move your eyes around.

    - Practice your enunciation and projection. Make each word clear, and speak at a volume that will reach the back row.

- Strive for a pace of about 100–150 words per minute—much slower than normal conversation. If pace is a problem for you, have a friend in the room who can silently signal "too fast" or "too slow" at presentation time.

- Pauses are a great way to create emphasis: "It's the fastest street-legal car … in the world." Conveniently, pauses can also give you time to adjust your pacing, take a calming breath, or avoid the dreaded "Um. … "

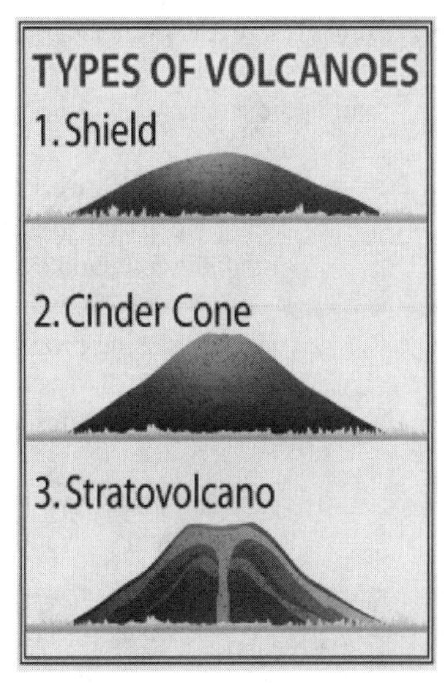

The best presentation posters are simple, with short, easy-to-read text and clear visuals.

- If you move around during your speech, move with purpose. Aimless pacing is distracting; moving from prop to prop, acting out scenarios, or interacting with audience members are all good reasons to move.

- Humor can keep your audience engaged, but keep it clean and use it with precision—another case where less is more.

- If you're really confident in your knowledge, leave time for questions and answers at the end of your presentation.

- When presenting in groups, carefully plan who is responsible for each section and what order members present in. Rehearse together, give each other feedback, and encourage each other.

- Humans are mostly visual creatures, so including strong visuals in your presentation can be one of the most effective ways to reach your audience.
    - Posters and PowerPoint slides should be simple and easy to read. Keep text to a minimum, use simple backgrounds and a readable font, and avoid clutter or fancy transitions.
    - If you're using props and demos, make sure to include them in your rehearsal sessions. Computer-animated demos can work well, if they're simple and clear.
    - Don't present to your slides, posters, or props. Keep your head up and facing the audience as much as possible.

Suggested Reading

Reynolds, *Presentation Zen*.

Tricks to Try

1. Theatrical improv is the ultimate challenge in off-the-cuff presentation. Ask your drama teacher for some improv exercises, or pick some games from your local comedy sports troupe or the television show *Who's Line Is It Anyway?* and play them with your friends. The results can be hilarious as well as good practice for giving presentations.

2. Practice your pacing, projection, enunciation, and tone by using a text you know well, like your favorite rap song. Count the number of words in the lyrics and try to hit a specific time. Grab an empty classroom at lunch hour, stick your friends in the back row, and recite it to them. Infuse your presentation with specific emotions using pauses, facial expressions, volume changes, and so on. For a real challenge, try displaying emotions at odds with the content; for example, if the song is about a party, try delivering it as if you're talking about a funeral.

Taking Control of Tests
Lecture 11

Topics in This Lecture

- Preparing for exams
- Test-taking strategies
- Learning from tests after you've taken them

Key Points

- Tests are only one way to measure your abilities, focusing on factual knowledge and analytical skills. If you judge your intelligence based on how you perform on school exams, you will either overestimate or underestimate your own intellect.

- Tests don't have to be something other people do to you. You can use tests to your advantage as a vehicle for learning and success. You'll need a strong work ethic and a dedication to good preparation.

- Cramming doesn't work. Spread out your study periods for at least a week before the exam. This gives you time to absorb the concepts more deeply and permanently and to ask your instructor questions in the days before the exam. The night before the exam, do a quick review and get a good night's rest.

- Good test prep begins with knowing the test format (multiple choice, fill in the blank, essay, etc.) so you won't be surprised; don't hesitate to ask your teacher. Also ask your teacher which are the most important concepts to review—notice, this isn't the same as asking, "What's going to be on the test?" Looking at previous tests from this class will give you clues about format and content as well.

- We can divide study strategies into three main areas: basic facts, big ideas, and application.

    - On most tests you'll need to know basic facts like vocabulary, names, dates, or formulas. You can learn these by rote memorization. Flash cards work well for studying these facts. Mnemonic acronyms and rhymes are good too.

    - The big ideas for the upcoming exam are sometimes posted on your classroom wall, summarized at the beginning or end of the chapter(s) in your textbook, or simply said by your teacher. If it's not clear by the time you start studying, ask. The big ideas determine which facts and details you need to study.

    - You'll need to practice application of both the big ideas and the facts. For example, in math classes, you'll want to do practice problems. For history or English, you'll need to practice writing essays.

- In each of your 20- to 30-minute study bursts, focus on a single concept, but approach it in multiple ways, so you're paving a variety of neural pathways with the same information.

- Group study can be effective, but all group members must be disciplined and focused, and you need to meet frequently enough to build habits and camaraderie. Try making up exam questions for each other, answering them separately, then meeting to review the answers. You can also give each other timed quizzes to practice your performance under pressure.

Different Questions, Different Strategies

You shouldn't approach different types of exam questions the same way. Here are some strategies for approaching some major question types:

- m**ultiple choice**: Read the instructions carefully. Are you choosing the best answer, picking out the one false answer, or what? When you read each question, try to answer it before you reading the possible answers. Next, read all of the answers before you make a decision. Eliminate the ones you're sure are wrong, then eliminate the distracters (true statements that don't quite answer the question). Hopefully, that will leave one answer standing—the right one.
- **matching**: Make the easy matches first so you have fewer options to choose from for the harder ones. Work both left-to-right and right-to-left; for example, don't just look at the definitions and try to find the word that fits, but also look at the words and see what definitions match the ones in your head. When you're down to the last few, don't get random. Really work the process of elimination to narrow down the possibilities.
- **fill in the blank:** Look around at other exam questions for hints, vocabulary words, and correct spelling.
- **essays**: Read the questions really carefully and know exactly what it's asking. If you're not sure, ask for clarification from the teacher. Before writing your answer, make an outline in a margin, on the back of the test, or on scratch paper. Once you do start writing, get to the point; don't waste time with fluff and style. Support each point with details. When you're done, reread your answer to make sure you've answered the specific question. Finally, if you run out of time, list the points you were going to make in outline style; you may get partial credit for them.

- Now it's test time! When you get the exam, don't just dive in. You need a strategy.
    - First, scan the whole test. This gives you an idea of the themes and concepts you'll need. You also may find answers to some questions within other questions.
    - Second, divide and conquer for time management. Figure out which sections will take the most and the least time, then plan accordingly.
    - Third, choose one of two plans of attack: Either work through the test section by section (easier for time management), or better yet, make two passes, answering the questions you know first and coming back to the ones you don't know. The latter allows you to build your confidence and gives you time to dig the harder answers out of your memory.

Group studying can be effective if everyone is focused. It helps if the group has a common purpose and a sense of camaraderie.

- Never skimp on reading the instructions! Not only can hints be hidden there, but what if the instructions say, "Answer one of the following essay questions," and you waste time answering all three? Then focus on just one question at a time —the one you're working on.

- Before you turn in your test, review your answers. Look for skipped problems. Make sure your answers are reasonable. But don't second guess yourself too much. Only change answers if you made an obvious mistake or something else on the test reminded you of the correct answer.

- It's not over when you turn the test in. When you get the test back, spend some time reviewing it, not just for the answers you missed but for how your teacher constructed the test. If the teacher reviews the test in class, take advantage of that time and ask good questions.

- If you disagree with how your test was graded, approach your teacher with—you know the drill—tact and respect. Let your teacher know that you're more concerned about what you can learn from your mistakes than about your grade.

Tricks to Try

1. Got test anxiety? You're not alone. The best way to ease your fears is to practice being tested. Make up a practice exam and take it under actual test conditions—sitting at a desk and with a time limit. Lots of people suffer from test anxiety, so don't beat yourself up. But if you've tried it all and it's still disrupting your grades—and even your health—talk to your parents, your teacher, or even your doctor. They want to help.

2. Where can you get practice questions to study from? Study buddies can write questions for each other if they know the material pretty well. If you have a learning center at your school, they may have practice exams. Your textbook will usually have some questions at the end of each chapter—your teacher may even use one of these on the test. When all else fails, go to the source: your teacher. He or she may have old exams for you to use or will know of other resources.

Finding Balance
Lecture 12

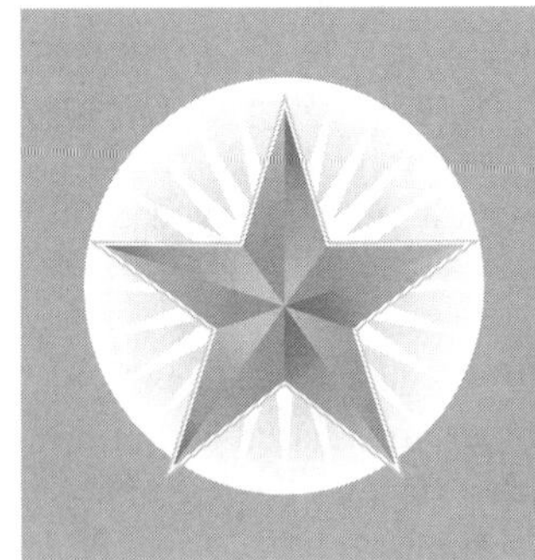

Topics in This Lecture

- Developing a balanced mind
- How to balance your time
- Course conclusion

Key Points

- A balanced mind and a balanced life are important. Your future employers and the colleges you apply to won't just be looking at your grades and test scores; they're going to consider your life skills and experiences. They want to know if you're creative, adaptable, motivated, passionate, and able to work with a team.

- You need balance for yourself as well. Having a fulfilling community life and personal life will make you a healthier, happier, and more interesting person; you'll also be a more successful friend, spouse, parent, neighbor, and citizen.

- The temple of the Oracle of Delphi, the most important shrine in ancient Greece, was inscribed with two words: "Know thyself." You need to assess yourself honestly, acknowledging both strengths and weaknesses. As you plan your future, you can play to your strengths, but you should also challenge yourself to work on your weaknesses.

  - If you're weak on creativity, find a way to be creative within your stronger areas. Mathematicians can try their hand at architecture. Computer programmers might take up Photoshop. Chemistry whizzes could apply their knowledge to cooking. And so on. The habit of creativity can then spill over into your school life.

  - If you lack practical skills, try classes at school or at the local rec center that let you work with your hands—a shop, agriculture, or home economics class, for example. Accepting a leadership position also helps you work on practical skills like planning and interpersonal skills. You could even start your own business.

  - It's becoming easier and easier to access facts online, and learning to find them with speed and precision is great. But that's really no substitute for having information in your own mind or via handheld devices. Understanding how facts fit on your tree of knowledge will help you retain the information, as will using the facts as often as possible.

- One of the biggest challenges you're probably facing right now—even if you're not aware of it—is how to balance school, work, and play. Balance in school starts with choosing the right classes. That means a variety of subjects, from core academics to art, technical, and gym classes. Choose classes that are interesting to you and some that will challenge you.

- Balancing your time outside school starts with the sort of goal planning we discussed early in the course. Plan ahead. Stay focused on all your goals.

- Work is an important part of growing up because it helps you build skills, responsibility, and a bank account. Working for others offers a steady paycheck, well-defined responsibilities, and maybe even mentorship. Starting your own business offers more risks, but it also helps you learn more diverse skills and may make you more money.

© Stockbyte/Thinkstock.

There's plenty to be learned outside the classroom. Having a job expands your horizons in countless ways.

- Volunteering and service work help you develop some skills, but it also gives back to the community, making your relationships stronger. And speaking of relationships, attending to your chores and to other family obligations will lead to more harmony and happiness at home.

- With all these demands and all this responsibility, it's important to remember that play is not an option; it's a necessity. Play can be organized like a school club, or it can be simple down time. You need some of both for your mental and physical health. If you can't make the time, it's okay to consider cutting back on other activities.

- If you can't seem to find the time to do what you need and want to do, the first thing to do is analyze how you spend your time now. You can track it on paper or use a phone app or your computer. Be honest; lying to yourself only hurts you. Once you have an idea of how much time you spend on each thing, you need to compare it against your goals and make some adjustments, either by changing the way you spend your time or setting more realistic goals.

- For more efficiency, try to overlap some of your activities. I'm not suggesting multitasking, but you can study flash cards while babysitting or listen to a podcast while mowing the lawn. Play and work can be combined too, if you can find a job doing what you love.

- Your time is valuable, so weigh each commitment you make carefully. Sometimes it's hard to say no, but if an obligation doesn't align with your goals or your schedule, learn to say no with our old friends politeness and tact. No elaborate excuses, no lies, just a gracious, complimentary no thank you.

- You should strive for quality in everything you do, but once in a while, it's okay to say, "Good enough." Sometimes staying up later to keep studying is counterproductive for example. Push yourself, but know when to cut yourself some slack.

- As long as the rest of your life is in balance, you should find one or two things that you really love to do, that you're passionate about, and that you have a talent for. Take those one or two things to a deeper level.

- Remember, school is not the same thing as education. School only lasts for a few years. Education happens all the time: before, during, and after school and for the rest of your life.

Suggested Reading

Csikszentmihalyi, *Flow*.

Gardner, *Five Minds for the Future*.

Goleman, *Emotional Intelligence*.

Robinson and Aronica, *The Element*.

Trick to Try

1. Draw your own unique Diamond Geisometer. Then take a look at those goals you set way back in Lecture 1. Do those goals help you balance out the diamond? If not, how can you tweak them to achieve better balance?

Parent Lecture Guides

Managing Your Child's Education

Parent's Lecture 1

Topics in This Lecture

- Teaching your children by being a learner yourself
- The importance of education outside of school
- The school's role in education

Key Points

- Ultimately, your child's education is up to your child. As parents, your job is to provide the best environment in which learning can take place, an environment where learning is valued, modeled, and celebrated by everyone. This means not only working with your child's teachers to reinforce the lessons in the classroom but also encouraging your children to pursue after-school activities that both play to their strengths and interests and shore up their weaknesses.

- For tens of thousands of years, parents have been the primary builders of their children's knowledge, skills, and beliefs. Only recently, in the past 200 years or so, has education become a formal institution. But just because the teachers are the professionals, we shouldn't simply turn our children's education over to them. You know your child best; you know your child's unique needs and talents better than anyone.

- A child who is inspired to learn will figure out the details along the way. Your role as a parent is to openly yearn for knowledge yourself. You can demonstrate this love of knowledge in many little ways, from the books you choose to read to joining your child in his or her hobbies and problem-solving tasks.

- Students only spend about 10 percent of their lives between birth and age 18 in school. But you shouldn't try to fill all their "spare" time with summer school classes, online study programs, and trips to museums. Unstructured play time helps children build collaborative, creative, and problem-solving skills more effectively than highly structured activities.

Are You Teaching Your Children to Love Learning?

At the end of the day, it's not always easy to muster the energy and enthusiasm for learning that your children need to see from you. But you don't need to put on a great show of scholarship at every family meal. You can demonstrate a commitment to knowledge in little ways every day. Ask yourself the following:

- How often do you ask questions of the people around you?
- How often do you say, "I'm not sure, but let's see if we can figure it out"?
- Are you reading books of substance, watching good documentaries, and discussing the world news in the evenings?
- Are you taking on new projects at work and excited about the challenges they bring?
- When was the last time you took a class to get better at something?
- How often do you tackle do-it-yourself projects instead of just hiring someone else to do it for you?
- Are you taking an interest in your child's activities and hobbies and learning about them, even if you don't find them very interesting?

- When deciding how to help round out your children's education, think about their strengths and their weakness, both in terms of learning styles and interests. Leisure activities should develop your child's natural strengths but also help shore up their weaknesses. Just don't try to control everything; let your children figure themselves out and pursue their passions.

- Humans are genetically wired for an extended period of childhood learning. We have incredibly adaptable, powerful, and creative brains, brains built for learning. But our natural classroom back on the African savannah was very unlike the modern school environment. Educators now recognize this, and schools are gradually changing, but fostering a more natural, skills-based environment outside the classroom will help your child do better inside the classroom.

- Even if you're overly busy with work, family, and other obligations—and who isn't these days—there are a few things you can do to support the teacher's efforts in the classroom. (We'll cover most of these in depth in later lectures.) Communicate with your child's teachers; learn how to help your child with homework without fights or doing it for them; and track your child's progress all the time, not just when report cards come out.

Suggested Reading

Csikszentmihalyi, *Flow*.

Louv, *Last Child in the Woods*.

Robinson and Aronica, *The Element*.

Tricks to Try

1. In Lecture 1 of the student section of this guidebook, your child is challenged to set goals for school and beyond. Encourage your child to complete the worksheet. Be there to address any questions and concerns he or she has while setting goals.

2. Make asking specific questions about what your children are learning in school a daily family ritual. It doesn't have to be a formal briefing; it can be a simple round-up over dessert.

Understanding How We Learn

Parent's Lecture 2

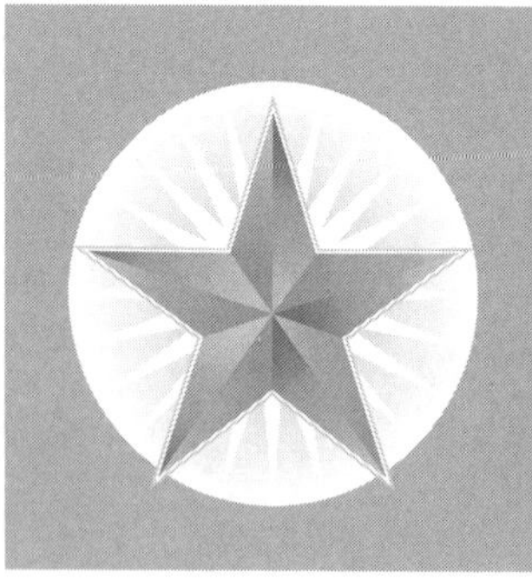

Topics in This Lecture

- How humans learn and assimilate new information
- How to stay at the forefront of your child's learning
- Working with different learning styles

Key Points

- We're going to be diving a bit deeper into some of the concepts that I presented in the students' Lectures 1 and 2. If you didn't watch those with your offspring, they might be worth checking out now.

- Your children learn from you, but you can actually learn from your children. They have a natural curiosity and are constantly picking up information. However, they don't organize information very well; that's one of the skills this course aims at teaching them.

- Some of the best times to check in with your children are when you're doing something active together, like hiking or biking. Exercise not only improves cognition, but having something to do together makes your questions seem less like interrogation and more like conversation as equals.

- Back in the first student session, I introduced the metaphor of a tree of knowledge: the leaves are pieces of information, and the branches are the framework of how we understand the world.

    - The younger the child, the simpler his or her knowledge tree. When he or she learns a new piece of information (say, for example, that a bird's nether region is called a vent), it probably gets placed on a pretty general branch of the trec (in this case, maybe under Nature > Birds > Body Parts).

    - The more a child learns, the more the tree branches. So encountered later in life, that bird vent might go under Sciences > Natural > Biology > Zoology > Birds > Anatomy > Digestive.

- As parents, you can use the tree metaphor to help your children organize the leaves on their trees. Specifically, you can help them with multiple encoding.

    - A piece of information isn't just stored in one place. Unlike a computer file—or a leaf on a tree—it can exist in many places, attached to many different branches at once.

    - When your child talks about information discussed in class or in a textbook, try to connect it to other information, either information from your life or your child's life, current events, movies, sports, whatever works. A leaf attached to two or more branches will be easier to retrieve when needed.

    - Making multiple associations also helps people understand relationships, underlying concepts, and the big picture behind what they're learning. Connecting a leaf to several seemingly unrelated branches can even stimulate creativity.

The Tree of Knowledge

1. **Sciences**
    a. Formal
        i. Math
        ii. Logic
    b. Natural
        i. Biology
            1. Botany
            2. Zoology
                a. Invertebrates
                b. Vertebrates
                    i. Fish
                    ii. Amphibians
                    iii. Reptiles
                    iv. Birds
                        1. Anatomy
                            a. Respiratory
                            b. Circulatory
                            c. **Digestive**
                                (the bird vent!)
                            d. Nervous
                            e. Reproductive
                            f. Skeletal-Muscular
                        2. Behavior
                        3. Ecology
                        4. Evolution
                    v. Mammals
            3. Microbiology
            4. Genetics
            5. Ecology
        ii. Chemistry
        iii. Physics
    c. Humanistic
        i. Psychology
        ii. Sociology

2. Humanities
    a. Language
        i. Grammar
        ii. World languages
        iii. Literature
    b. History
        i. Pre-history
        ii. Eastern
        iii. Western
        iv. Modern
    c. The arts
        i. Visual
        ii. Performing
    d. Philosophy
        i. Secular
        ii. Religious

Your child's tree of knowledge becomes more and more complex as he or she ages, matures, and learns.

- The zone of proximal development (ZPD) is the realm of learning that exists just outside the boundary of your child's current knowledge and skills. If new ideas and concepts are too difficult, they're outside the ZPD and outside the student's reach. If the new ideas are too easy, then the student isn't pushing the boundary and growing.

- One clue that your child's schoolwork is outside his or her ZPD is boredom, restlessness, and refusal to complete work. As a parent, your job is to notice this, figure out whether the work is too hard or too easy. If it's too hard, your task is to give your child the knowledge and skills to bridge the gap. If it's too easy, you can challenge your child at home, or you can talk to your child's teacher about options for more advanced work.

- When your child's work is outside your ZPD (or exists on branches of your knowledge tree that have withered and died), be willing to become a fellow student. Learning the material together not only helps your child achieve; it sets a good example of lifelong learning.

- Psychologist Howard Gardner describes seven different intelligences, or learning styles: logical/mathematical, linguistic/verbal, visual/spatial, musical, kinesthetic, interpersonal, and intrapersonal. All of us possess each faculty in some measure and are dominant in two or three of them. But traditional education only measures and rewards logical/mathematical and linguistic/verbal learning.

- Your child needs to know his or her own thinking and learning styles to achieve. There are many online tools to help you with this, as well as a quiz at the back of this guidebook. In the student section of this course, I've offered lots of tips for working with different learning styles, and plenty of excellent books exist to help you help your child go even further.

- It's important to reinforce to your children that they're unique and that that's okay, regardless of how they are labeled by an IQ test, a grade point average, or a standardized assessment. A discouraged learner is an ineffective learner, so build your children up by focusing on what they're good at, but also supporting them in the areas where they need help.

Suggested Reading

Gardner, *Art, Mind, and Brain*.

Quiroga et al., "Explicit Encoding of Multimodal Percepts by Single Neurons in the Human Brain."

———, "Invariant Visual Representation by Single Neurons in the Human Brain."

Tricks to Try

1. Challenge your child to a branch off. Pick a subject or concept he or she is currently studying and take turns connecting that concept to more and more branches of knowledge. There are no wrong answers. No connection is out of bounds. Get playful with it!

2. When discussing schoolwork with your children, ask them open-ended questions, rather than quizzing them and expecting specific answers. Open-ended questions allow them to prove they understand (or don't understand) the underlying concepts, not just a string of facts.

Helping with Homework

Parent's Lecture 3

Topics in This Lecture

- Creating an environment for homework success
- How to help, and how not to help, with your child's homework
- What to do when things get tough

Key Points

- Homework doesn't need to be a battle. It doesn't need to be last minute. It doesn't need to be painful. Too often, we treat homework like it's a punishment, fostering an unhealthy attitude toward learning. If we want our children to develop into responsible, self-motivated, long-term learners, we need to help them discover the joy of learning at home.

- The first step is creating an environment for success. That means setting the mood, organizing spaces, and scheduling times for your child's homework.

- In response to a stressful event, the body's adrenal glands release adrenaline and cortisol. Cortisol affects the hippocampus and actually reduces your ability to create short-term or long-term memories. Therefore, it's important to reduce unnecessary stress in a student's study environment. Students should feel challenged and alert but not under threat.

- Reduced stress doesn't mean no consequences. Clearly lay out the consequences for not doing homework or not doing it well. When your child shirks homework, follow up calmly, unemotionally, and according to the rules you laid out, and then back off. No temper, no overkill. Your children need to feel that your response was reasonable and just.

- Students need a physical environment that's conducive to studying. I gave the students some ideas about this in Lecture 5, but as the head of the household, you should help them set up spaces that allow them to focus and give them the tools and supplies they need to succeed. Help your children set up their spaces, but let them decorate the spaces and make them their own.

- Minimize distractions during homework time. Turn off media, spend time with the little ones if they're fussy, and avoid interrupting your student for non-homework-related reasons (except, of course, dinner).

Getting Unstuck

What can you do if your child is completely stuck and you're unable to help?

- Look for other resources. Your child's textbook should have plenty of information, including practice questions and further resources. Many textbook publishers offer online supplements to their books as well, not to mention all those teachers who've built great websites with lots of information.

- Find experts you know for the subjects you don't know. Relatives, neighbors, colleagues, friends, and even your child's classmates can all be valuable resources when you and your child are in over your heads.

- Your child's school may have tutors, mentors, and counselors available. If the going gets really tough, consider a private tutor.

Keep in mind, you have your own areas of expertise. Consider offering yourself as a tutor or mentor at your child's school.

- Students need help establishing a schedule and routine. Just like you need to unwind after coming home from the office, they need to unwind after a long day at school, so make sure leisure time is part of the schedule. Schedules should also be flexible enough to adapt to changing activities and priorities throughout the school year. Review Lecture 4 of the students' section for more tips.

- It can be helpful to sct a minimum amount of time for homework each night. When kids say "I don't have any homework" or "I did it all at school," it can be code for "I don't want to do my homework." If they know they have to spend, say, at least 30 minutes on homework anyway, they're more likely to soldier up and do it.

- Set time limits for computer use, television watching, phone calls, and other teenage pursuits. Also, at the start of each school year, set bedtimes for both weekdays and weekends. Adolescents are growing rapidly both physically and mentally. They need sleep to repair muscles and consolidate all their new knowledge.

- We want to develop responsible and autonomous offspring; responsibility and autonomy don't happen by themselves. When it comes to homework, therefore, you need to find the right balance between autonomy and accountability.

- Be accessible while your child is working, but don't hover. Offer to help if they're stuck. Offer to help with flash cards and practice quizzes. Offer to proofread or check over their work when they're done. But don't force it; just offer.

- It's okay to help, but don't try to fix all of your child's work. Kids do learn from their mistakes, and teachers need an honest assessment of your child's progress. Help should come in the form of structure and support, not direct intervention.

- Sometimes kids get frustrated and angry, and sometimes we just don't know how to help. You know your child better than anyone, and you're best at recognizing the tipping point between normal frustration and the verge of meltdown. When meltdown threatens, take a break with your child. Do something physical together to burn off those stress hormones so he or she can calm down.

- When your child is ready to work again, try switching to a subject he or she is more skilled in. This will help build confidence back up and give your child a cleaner slate to start from when returning to the tough stuff.

- When all else fails, don't be afraid to let your child call it quits for the night and write a note for them to bring to the teacher. But save this option for real emergencies. Then follow up with the teacher about the sort of assistance your child will need to make up the work and avoid further problems.

Tricks to Try

1. Give plenty of praise to your kids when they do a good job, whether on the quality of their homework or for simply being responsible and getting it done on their own. Be specific with your praise: "Nice work on this project. It looks great!" "I'm proud of you for planning ahead on that long paper!" If you do find something to correct, offer constructive feedback rather than criticism or teasing.

2. One of the best things you can do to improve your child's homework environment is to work on homework yourself at the same time. Pay the bills, do some work you brought home from the office, write thank you notes, or simply grab a book and read. Not only will you minimize distractions and get something done, but you'll also model the ability to focus, have discipline, and engage in lifelong learning.

Working with Teachers

Parent's Lecture 4

Topics in This Lecture

- Foundations of the parent-teacher relationship
- Three-way communication
- Handling problems and complaints

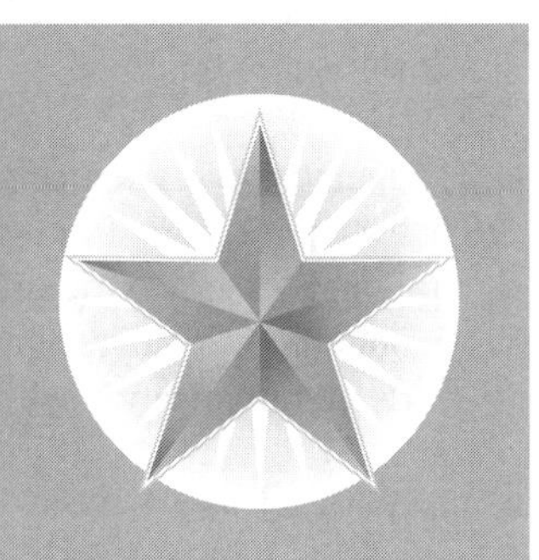

Key Points

- The foundations of your relationship with your child's teacher are the same as just about any relationship: respect and understanding. Teaching is an exhausting but rewarding profession, and teachers' work is often misunderstood and underappreciated. So the first step to a good relationship with a teacher is to respect his or her abilities, judgment, and professionalism.

- Respect begins with respectful language. Just thanking the teacher or saying you appreciate his oe her hard work will get you off on the right foot. Also, showing respect for your child's teachers sets an example for your children, and they'll be more likely to be respectful, too.

- Understanding your child's teacher means recognizing that teaching, like learning and parenting, exists within a much larger system. Just as you have constraints on how you raise your children such as time, money, and other obligations, so too do teachers have limitations on how and what they teach their students.

- Middle and high school teachers singlehandedly work with more than 100 students a day on average; in some schools, class lists approach 200 students every day. Keep this in mind when making requests for your child. Most teachers are happy to give a student individual support, but it may need to occur at lunch or after school rather than during class time.

- In many schools, especially larger secondary schools, communication between teachers from one year to the next is unfortunately pretty minimal. Also, we too often rely on our children as the communication conduit between ourselves and their teachers. That's where establishing early communication with your child's teacher comes in.

- It's a good idea to open communications with your child's teacher as soon as possible. Establish contact with teachers within the first couple of weeks each fall, in person if possible, and with your child present; the teacher will remember you better that way, and your child will see that you're interested and engaged with their education.

- The first meeting is a good time to find out what each teacher's preferred method of contact is—phone, e-mail, or face-to-face. Dropping in without an appointment is rarely a good idea, unless the teacher has specific open office hours.

- Before meeting with the teacher, do your research. Many schools keep parents informed with newsletters, website updates, and the like. Your child's school likely has a handbook, and you can look at your child's syllabus and textbook for a good grasp of what's going on in class.

- If effective communication with a teacher breaks down, or you have serious questions about something a teacher is doing, it's important to approach the situation calmly and with an open mind. Talk to your child first in a respectful, non-confrontational way. If you think you need the teacher's side of the story, for minor issues it might be enough to call or e-mail. For bigger or recurring issues, a face-to-face meeting may be better.

- To meet with a teacher, call or e-mail ahead of time to set up an appointment and to let the teacher know (1) what you want to talk about and (2) whether or not your child will be in the meeting. In the vast majority of cases, it's best include the student so he or she feels included and can take an active role in resolving the problem.

- Approach the meeting knowing that everyone wants to help your child be successful, even your child. Always open the meeting with positive things, things that are working, and try to finish up the meeting the same way, no matter how tough the issues in the middle are to discuss.

- Although it may be hard to let go of control, ultimately, the solution to any problem in school will rest squarely on the student's shoulders. Teachers, parents, and other adults can support them, but if we want our children to mature and become more responsible, we need to leave the bulk of the work up to them, even if this means letting your child experience failure.

- When a plan of action is reached, write down the details (including milestones and consequences) and make sure you, your child, and the teacher each have a copy. Check in with your child a few days in to make sure the plan is on track, then step back for about a month and let your child take the reins. If the situation isn't improving by then, it may be time to revisit the plan.

- On the rare occasion when all evidence says the teacher is behaving unreasonably or uncooperatively, the first step is to go to the teacher directly. Don't go over the teacher's head as the first resort. Remember to start and end the conversation with something positive. When you do bring up your concern, do so in a way that focuses on solutions.

Tricks to Try

1. One great way to build a good relationship with teachers and administrators at your child's school is to volunteer. Not every parent has the resources to get involved, but if you do, it's a great way to serve your family and the community. Opportunities of all sizes abound, from regular commitments like coaching and scouting to one-off commitments like career days and in-class demonstrations. Think about your schedule and what talents you could bring to the table.

2. The positive communication "sandwich" isn't just for dealing with teachers. Take note of how you communicate with your family members, co-workers, and neighbors. If you started and ended every serious talk with positive comments, do you think the outcomes would improve?

Preparing for College and the Future

Parent's Lecture 5

Topics in This Lecture

- What you can do to help your child prepare for college and the future
- The best and worst ways to prepare and apply to college
- The predictors for success in college

Key Points

- About 40 percent of students have to take remedial classes in college, and most of these students had good grades in high school. Although these students learned a lot about academic subjects, no one had taught them how to work hard, how to study, or how to learn. Fortunately, you can make sure this isn't your child's story.

- A young adult often doesn't make a final career choice during their postsecondary education. College or vocational school is just one step on a continuous journey of lifelong learning. Most of the careers your children will pursue haven't even been invented yet. Think about it: Were there search engine optimization specialists or professional bloggers when you were in school?

- During the high school years, having some general goals is more important than setting a rigid career plan. Your child should revisit these goals often and, with your help, revise them as he or she grows and matures.

- As you speak about college with your children, don't simply relate it to getting a better job. College is also about educating individuals to make a difference in every aspect of their lives and communities, to develop involved citizens and a creative individuals who are well-rounded, personally satisfied, and socially minded citizens.

- Public and private four-year universities are a great choice for many students, and in general, they offer a broad liberal arts education plus the opportunity to specialize in one or more areas. But they are not the

What Are Colleges Looking For?

The most selective colleges have their pick of outstanding students to choose from, sometimes 10 or 20 applicants for every seat. Colleges are looking for well-rounded students, but they're also looking for a well-rounded overall student body. For the most part, these factors will be out of your control.

Ultimately, trying to figure out what will make *that one school* accept your child is a futile exercise. A well-balanced student will find a great fit. Some general criteria for achieving balance are as follows:

All colleges value ...	Some colleges also look for ...
rigorous class choices	a strong application essay
class rank	outstanding recommendations
high or steadily rising GPA	leadership experience
Strong SAT and/or ACT scores	evidence of good character
evidence of a good work ethic outside school (extracurriculars, sports, jobs, volunteer work, etc.)	evidence of time-management skills and other indicators of maturity

only options for career success and personal fulfillment. An art or design school prepares creative individuals for competitive media careers. Vocational schools are a good option for people with aptitude in a particular technical discipline.

- For some, particularly those on a budget, a two-year community college degree can stand on its own, or the credits can be transferred to a four-year college that would otherwise be financially out of reach. But if your child has set sights on a private four-year school, scholarships and aid are available for all kinds of students based on all kinds of criteria for those willing to hunt for them.

- When saving for college, don't just tuck the money away and never say anything about it. Talk with your children about how your family is going to pay for their post-secondary education. Students should have a role in planning ahead, saving, and working to help fund their own education.

- You might be surprised that good grades and standardized test scores are not the best predictor of college success. The biggest predictor is a student's conscientiousness—dependability, perseverance, and work ethic. Agreeableness, teamwork, and emotional balance play a large role as well.

- Most of the college application process takes place in the student's junior and senior years. It's important to make this process the child's responsibility. It's okay to help—particularly with remembering deadlines, visiting schools, and attending college fairs—but don't do the work for them.

- While you might have some strong opinions about where your child should go to school, ultimately the postsecondary path has to be your child's own path. You can buy them school apparel, and you can leave brochures lying around for them to notice, but don't force them to follow in your footsteps.

Suggested Reading

Gardner, *Five Minds for the Future*.

Tricks to Try

1. Brochures are great, but when it comes to learning about a college, nothing beats hearing about students' personal experiences. Campus visits where your child gets to spend a day with a current student will give them a great feel for what to expect at that school. You can also contact older alumni to find out how they see their alma mater in hindsight.

2. Modern college admissions boards don't just look at grades but at a student's school activities, volunteer work, and paid employment. That doesn't mean, however, that your child should do everything that fits into his or her schedule. Quality over quantity: Deep involvement and leadership in one or two activities is more impressive than being jack of all trades and master of none.

Parenting with Balance

Parent's Lecture 6

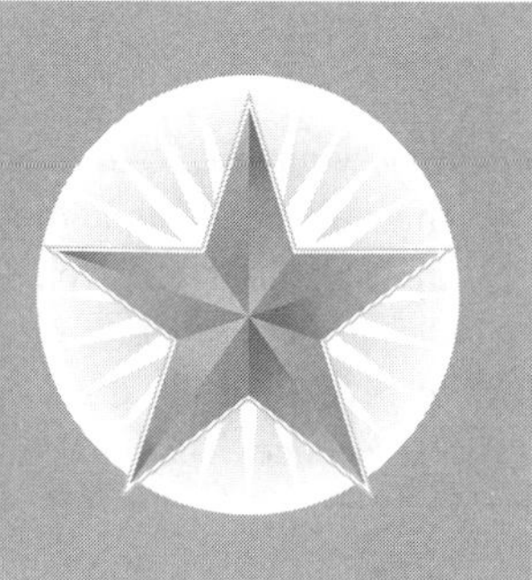

Topic in This Lecture

- What it means to parent with balance from a teacher's perspective

Key Points

- Teachers not only teach; they step into the roles of psychologist, pediatrician, child-development specialist, and even parent to their students. While you know your child best and are your child's primary teacher for the most important developmental years of his or her life, teachers have a unique perspective on what your child-as-student needs from you.

- Your main role is not to force the learning to happen; it's to inspire your child to learn. If you build your child's educational home without inspiring them, including them in the decisions, or teaching them how to build an educational home themselves, it's not going to last.

- As you move forward, be sure to do so with the goals that your child developed at the beginning of this course. I recommend hanging them somewhere prominent in your home. If your kids are too embarrassed to have them hanging on the fridge, put them on the inside of a cupboard or closet door—out of plain sight but regularly seen anyway.

- Try to set some goals for yourself in these same (or similar) categories that your student did. Not only is that a good idea for you as a person, but it's also important for your kids to see the adults in their lives setting goals and striving toward them. Remember too that goal lists are living documents. Revisit them and adapt them as your child grows older or as circumstances change.

- Ask yourself, "Am I enrolling my children in activities that I want them to do or that they want to do?" Be wary of living vicariously through your children. If your child isn't enjoying what he or she is doing, perhaps it's time to back out. On the other hand, don't be afraid to give your children a gentle push toward expanding their skills and experiences—a *gentle* push, not a shove off a cliff.

- Some parents argue that if their son or daughter emerges from school as a successful student, gets into a great university, and launches a wildly successful career, it doesn't matter if they don't have a good relationship with their own child. But the truth is, the strength of your relationship with your children actually increases their chances of success—especially in the areas of happiness and personal fulfillment.

- We need to be careful with the language we use around our children and about our children. We're all guilty of talking about "dealing" with our children, as if it were some sort of ordeal, rather than a loving relationship. Some of us talk about our kids in the third person, even when they're right there in the room. Look at your language carefully, listen to the subtle messages it sends to your kids, and then work to improve it.

- Parents need to be willing to let their children fail. They need to experience the natural consequences of their actions. That doesn't mean letting your kids run wild and free. Set firm boundaries, but give your children plenty of room within them to explore, try new things, and sometimes even fail.

- Most of the time when your child asks for your help, it's better to offer guidance or a suggestion than a fix. Start giving children little responsibilities at an early age and increase them as they mature. Hold them to promises; enforce or let the school enforce just consequences for not meeting goals. Kids in this environment develop into responsible, mature, and creative adults that can take care of themselves.

- While you're looking around for parenting ideas, look for places where you can help others. Many parents struggling through their children's teenage years and would love some advice, some help, or maybe just someone to talk to. Many children don't have the kind of support you offer your kids. Getting involved in the world beyond your front door will not only help your kids and their friends grow; it will also enrich your life.

Suggested Reading

Cline and Fay, *Parenting Teens with Love and Logic.*

Csikszentmihalyi, *Flow.*

Gardner, *Five Minds for the Future.*

Goleman, *Emotional Intelligence.*

———, *Social Intelligence.*

Louv, *Last Child in the Woods.*

Robinson and Aronica, *The Element.*

Tricks to Try

1. If you haven't already, check out the goals spreadsheet in Lecture 1 of the student section of this guidebook and develop your own goals. Make self-improvement a family project.

2. How well do you know the parents of your child's friends? The next time your children are hanging out together, invite the adults over for coffee and get to know each other. Strengthening those relationships will help strengthen your own support system during the trying teenage years.

Multiple Intelligences Survey

This quick quiz will give you a good idea about your learning styles. Remember, everyone has some measure of all seven intelligences. You can strengthen each intelligence; knowing your intelligence type is meant to empower you, not label you. This inventory is also a snapshot in time. Your strengths and weaknesses can change.

PART I

Complete each section by placing a 1 next to each statement you feel accurately describes you. If you do not identify with a statement, leave the space blank. Then total the column in each section.

Section 1

_____ I easily pick up on patterns.

_____ I focus in on noise and sounds.

_____ Moving to a beat is easy for me.

_____ I enjoy making music.

_____ I respond to the cadence of poetry.

_____ I remember things by putting them in a rhyme.

_____ Concentration is difficult for me if there is background noise.

_____ Listening to nature sounds can be very relaxing.

_____ Musicals are more engaging to me than dramatic plays.

_____ Remembering song lyrics is easy for me.

_____ TOTAL for Section 1

Section 2

_____ I am known for being neat and orderly.

_____ Step-by-step directions are a big help.

_____ Problem solving comes easily to me.

_____ I get easily frustrated with disorganized people.

_____ I can complete calculations quickly in my head.

_____ Logic puzzles are fun.

_____ I can't begin an assignment until I have all my ducks in a row.

_____ Structure is a good thing.

_____ I enjoy troubleshooting something that isn't working properly.

_____ Things have to make sense to me or I am dissatisfied.

_____ TOTAL for Section 2

Section 3

_____ I learn best by interacting with others.

_____ I enjoy informal chat and serious discussion.

_____ The more the merrier.

_____ I often serve as a leader among peers and colleagues.

_____ I value relationships more than ideas or accomplishments.

_____ Study groups are very productive for me.

_____ I am a team player.

_____ Friends are important to me.

_____ I belong to more than three clubs or organizations.

_____ I dislike working alone.

_____ TOTAL for Section 3

Section 4

_____ I learn by doing.

_____ I enjoy making things with my hands.

_____ Sports are a part of my life.

_____ I use gestures and nonverbal cues when I communicate.

_____ Demonstrating is better than explaining.

_____ I love to dance.

_____ I like working with tools.

_____ Inactivity can make me more tired than being very busy.

_____ Hands-on activities are fun.

_____ I live an active lifestyle.

_____ TOTAL for Section 4

Section 5

_____ Foreign languages interest me.

_____ I enjoy reading books, magazines, and websites.

_____ I keep a journal.

_____ Word puzzles like crosswords or jumbles are enjoyable.

_____ Taking notes helps me remember and understand.

_____ I faithfully contact friends through letters and/or e-mail.

_____ It is easy for me to explain my ideas to others.

_____ I write for pleasure.

_____ Puns, anagrams, and spoonerisms are fun.

_____ I enjoy public speaking and participating in debates.

_____ TOTAL for Section 5

Section 6

_____ My attitude affects how I learn.

_____ I like to be involved in causes that help others.

_____ I am keenly aware of my moral beliefs.

_____ I learn best when I have an emotional attachment to the subject.

_____ Fairness is important to me.

_____ Social justice issues interest me.

_____ Working alone can be just as productive as working in a group.

_____ I need to know why I should do something before I agree to do it.

_____ When I believe in something, I give more effort toward it.

_____ I am willing to protest or sign a petition to right a wrong.

_____ TOTAL for Section 6

Section 7

_____ I can visualize ideas in my mind.

_____ Rearranging a room and redecorating are fun for me.

_____ I enjoy creating my own works of art.

_____ I remember better when using graphic organizers.

_____ I enjoy all kinds of entertainment media.

_____ Charts, graphs, and tables help me interpret data.

_____ A music video can make me more interested in a song.

_____ I can recall things as mental pictures.

_____ I am good at reading maps and blueprints.

_____ Three-dimensional puzzles are fun.

_____ TOTAL for Section 7

PART II

Fill out the table below with your total points from each section and multiply each total by 10.

Section	Total Forward	Multiply	Score
1		× 10	
2		× 10	
3		× 10	
4		× 10	
5		× 10	
6		× 10	
7		× 10	

PART III

Plot your scores on the following bar graph:

100							
90							
80							
70							
60							
50							
40							
30							
20							
10							
0	Sec. 1	Sec. 2	Sec. 3	Sec. 4	Sec. 5	Sec. 6	Sec. 7

Section 1 suggests your musical strength.

Section 2 indicates your logical/mathematical strength.

Section 3 shows your interpersonal strength.

Section 4 suggests your kinesthetic strength.

Section 5 indicates your linguistic/verbal strength.

Section 6 reflects your intrapersonal strength.

Section 7 suggests your visual/spatial strength.

You can find a detailed explanation of each of these intelligence types on p. 5–6.

Adapted from McKenzie, Walter: *The One and Only Surfaquarium*. http://surfaquarium.com/

Bibliography

Baggini, Julian, and Peter S. Fosl. *The Philosopher's Toolkit: A Compendium of Philosophical Concepts and Methods.* 2nd ed. Oxford: Wiley-Blackwell, 2010. An introduction to philosophy and the logical fallacies often present in poor critical thinking.

Bishop, J., C. Carter, and S. Kravits. *Keys to College Studying: Becoming an Active Thinker*. 2nd ed. Upper Saddle River, NJ: Pearson/Prentice Hall, 2007. A systemic and practical guide to developing the habits needed for success in college.

Clegg, Brian, and Paul Birch. *Instant Creativity: Simple Techniques to Ignite Innovation and Problem Solving*. London: Kogan Page, 2007. Full of techniques for divergent thinking and creative solutions.

Cline, Foster, and Jim Fay. *Parenting Teens with Love and Logic*. Colorado Springs: NavPress, 2006. A wonderful resource for parents who want to help their teenagers become independent and responsible decision makers.

Colvin, Geoffrey. *Talent is Overrated: What Really Separates World-Class Performers from Everybody Else*. New York: Portfolio, 2008. Colvin extols the virtues of hard work and perseverance, focusing on how to systematically get better at anything you do.

Csikszentmihalyi, Mihaly. *Flow: The Psychology of Optimal Experience*. New York: Harper Perennial, 2008. A research-based treatment of being "in the zone," a state of flow where time ceases to matter. This state is achieved when your skill level and the challenge you are faced with are high and leads to deep satisfaction.

Gardner, Howard. *Art, Mind, and Brain: A Cognitive Approach to Creativity*. New York: Basic Books, 1982. The landmark book where Gardner deconstructs our simplistic notion of intelligence and introduces his seven intelligences.

———. *Five Minds for the Future*. Boston: Harvard Business School Press, 2007. One of Gardner's more recent works focusing on the five "minds" needed for success in the future: disciplined, synthesizing, creative, respectful, and ethical.

Gelb, Michael. *Think like Da Vinci: 7 Easy Steps to Boosting Everyday Genius*. London: HarperElement, 2009. A practical guide with exercises to help anyone be more creative and innovative in their thinking.

Goleman, Daniel. *Emotional Intelligence: Why It Can Matter More Than IQ*. London: Bloomsbury, 2010. Goleman argues that emotional intelligence is perhaps a better predictor of future success than more traditional measures of intelligence.

———. *Social Intelligence: The New Science of Human Relationships*. New York: Bantam Books, 2006. Drawing from the field of social neuroscience, Goleman illustrates that our relationships actually shape our biology, and our lives.

Kaufman, James C., and Elena L. Grigorenko. *The Essential Sternberg: Essays on Intelligence, Psychology, and Education*. New York: Springer, 2009. An overview of Sternberg's work regarding intelligence and learning.

Louv, Richard. *Last Child in the Woods: Saving Our Children from Nature-Deficit Disorder*. Revised and updated ed. Chapel Hill, NC: Algonquin Books of Chapel Hill, 2008. A call for parents to let children be children, allowing for unstructured play and more connections with the natural world.

McDonald, Marcy. *Writing, the Bridge Between Us: A Step-by-Step Guide to Writing Well*. South Hill, VA: Popular Weasel Press, 2001. A complete and practical guide for the writer, complete with exercises and numerous examples.

McInerny, Dennis Q. *Being Logical: A Guide to Good Thinking*. New York: Random House, 2004. An accessible introduction to critical thinking and logical, reasoned debate.

Medina, John. *Brain Rules: 12 Principles for Surviving and Thriving at Work, Home, and School*. Seattle, WA: Pear Press, 2008. Medina draws upon the latest neuroscience to explain how we learn and the implications for each of us.

Newport, Cal. *How to Become a Straight-A Student: The Unconventional Strategies Real College Students Use to Score High while Studying Less*. New York: Broadway Books, 2007. A comprehensive guide to what great college students do to ensure success.

Pink, Daniel H. *A Whole New Mind: Why Right-Brainers Will Rule the Future*. New York: Riverhead Books, 2006. This book paints a new paradigm for the future, and argues that both sides of the brain will be necessary in the rapidly changing 21st century.

Pinker, Steven. *How the Mind Works*. New York: Norton, 1997. Pinker draws upon neuroscience and evolutionary biology to explain how the human mind works.

Quiroga, R. Quian, A. Kraskov, C. Koch, and I. Fried. "Explicit Encoding of Multimodal Percepts by Single Neurons in the Human Brain." *Current Biology* 19, no. 15 (2009): 1308–1313. doi:10.1016/j.cub.2009.06.060.

Quiroga, R. Quian, L. Reddy, G. Kreiman, C. Koch, and I. Fried. "Invariant Visual Representation by Single Neurons in the Human Brain." *Nature* 435 no. 7045 (2005): 1102-1107. doi:10.1038/nature3687.

Reynolds, Garr. *Presentation Zen: Simple Ideas on Presentation Design and Delivery*. Berkeley, CA: New Riders, 2008. The definitive guide to great presentations.

Robinson, Adam. *What Smart Students Know: Maximum Grades, Optimum Learning, Minimum Time*. New York: Crown Trade Paperbacks, 1993. A pragmatic guide to success in all areas of formal schooling.

Robinson, Ken. *Out of Our Minds: Learning to Be Creative*. Fully revised and updated ed. Oxford: Capstone, 2011. A thorough and fascinating treatise on creativity from one of the leading minds in innovative thinking.

Robinson, Ken, and Lou Aronica. *The Element: How Finding Your Passion Changes Everything*. New York: Penguin, 2009. This book considers the lives of successful people who have followed their passion and made a life out of it.

Rosen, Christine. "The Myth of Multitasking." *The New Atlantis* 20 (Spring 2008): 105–110. Debunks the idea that multitasking is a more efficient way to operate.

Sternberg, Robert J. *Successful Intelligence: How Practical and Creative Intelligence Determine Success in Life*. New York: Simon & Schuster, 1996. Sternberg argues that success in life is often determined by different types of intelligence than success in school.

Internet Resources

Bregman, Peter. "How (and Why) to Stop Multitasking." *Harvard Business Review*, May 20, 2010. http://blogs.hbr.org/bregman/2010/05/how-and-why-to-stop-multitaski.html.

Carey, Benedict. "Forget What You Know about Good Study Habits." *The New York Times*, Sepember 7, 2010. http://www.nytimes.com/2010/09/07/health/views/07mind.html?_r=2&pagewanted=all.

Colvin, Geoffrey. "What It Takes to Be Great." *CNNMoney*, October 19, 2006. http://money.cnn.com/magazines/fortune/fortune_archive/2006/10/30/8391794/index.htm.

"Fallacies." *The Writing Center, University of North Carolina at Chapel Hill*. http://www.unc.edu/depts/wcweb/handouts/fallacies.html.

"'Infomania' Worse than Marijuana." *BBC News*, April 22, 2005. http://news.bbc.co.uk/2/hi/uk_news/4471607.stm.

Jones-Kavalier, Barbara R., and Suzanne L. Flannigan. "Connecting the Digital Dots: Literacy of the 21st Century." *Educause Quarterly*, 29, no. 2 (2006). http://www.educause.edu/EDUCAUSE+Quarterly/EDUCAUSEQuarterlyMagazineVolum/ConnectingtheDigitalDotsLitera/157395.

"Most Students in Remedial Classes in College Had Solid Grades in High School, Survey Finds." *The Chronicle of Higher Education*, September 15, 2008. http://chronicle.com/article/Most-Students-in-Remedial/41611.

Naish, John. "Is Multi-Tasking Bad for Your Brain? Experts Reveal the Hidden Perils of Juggling Too Many Jobs." *The Daily Mail*, August 11, 2009. http://www.dailymail.co.uk/health/article-1205669/Is-multi-tasking-bad-brain-Experts-reveal-hidden-perils-juggling-jobs.html.

Ophir, Eyal, Clifford Nass, and Anthony D. Wagner. "Cognitive Control in Media Multitaskers." *Proceedings of the National Academy of Sciences*. Published online before print, August 24, 2009. doi:10.1073/pnas.0903620106.

Schwarz, Christina. "Leave Those Kids Alone." *The Atlantic*, April 2011. http://www.theatlantic.com/magazine/archive/2011/04/leave-those-kids-alone/8398.

Smith, Tovia. "Behind the Scenes: How Do You Get into Amherst?" *NPR*, March 28, 2011. http://www.npr.org/2011/03/28/134916924/Amherst-Admissions-Process?ft=1&f=1013

———. "What's New in High School? Stress Reduction 101." *NPR*, January 3, 2011. http://www.npr.org/2011/01/03/132630439/whats-new-in-high-school-stress-reduction-101?ft=1&f=1013.

"Think You Know How to Study? Think Again. *NPR*, October 21, 2010. http://www.npr.org/templates/story/story.php?storyId=130728588&ft=1&f=1013.

"Thinking Critically about Web 2.0 and Beyond" *UCLA Library, College Library Research Help, How-to Guides*. http://www.library.ucla.edu/libraries/college/11605_12008.cfm

Notes

Notes

Notes

Notes

Notes

Notes

Notes